Name That Bird

BIRDS&BLOOMS

Name That Bird

A Simple Approach to Identifying Your Backyard Friends

Reader's
Digest

The Reader's Digest Association, Inc.
New York, NY/Montreal

Copyright © 2011 The Reader's Digest Association, Inc.

Editor: Barbara Booth
Designer: Elizabeth Tunnicliffe
Senior Art Director: George McKeon
Executive Editor, Trade Publishing: Dolores York
Manufacturing Manager: Elizabeth Dinda
Associate Publisher, Trade Publishing: Rosanne McManus
President and Publisher, Trade Publishing: Harold Clarke

Library of Congress Cataloging-in-Publication Data

Name that bird : a simple approach to identifying your backyard friends / by editors at Birds and blooms.
    p. cm.
Includes index.
ISBN 978-1-60652-335-3
1. Birds--Identification. I. Reader's Digest Association. II. Birds & blooms.
QL673.N26 2011
598.01'2--dc22
2011003911

We are committed to both the quality of our products and the service we provide to our customers.
We value your comments, so please feel free to contact us.

The Reader's Digest Association, Inc.
Adult Trade Publishing
44 S. Broadway
White Plains, NY 10601

For more Reader's Digest products and information, visit our website:
www.rd.com (in the United States)
www.readersdigest.ca (in Canada)

Credits: Illustrations © The Reader's Digest Association, Inc./GID;
    photography © Shutterstock; iStockphoto: 69 *(right)*, 75 *(middle)*, 86 *(left)*, 112 *(left)*

Printed in China

1 3 5 7 9 10 8 6 4 2

I never for a day gave up listening to the songs of our birds, or watching their peculiar habits, or delineating them in the best way I could.

—John James Audubon

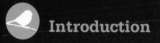

Introduction

Birds have a way of holding us captive in their magical spell. They please us with their willingness to come to feeders, impress us with their preoccupation with nest and nestlings, astound us with their courtship displays, and amaze us with their miraculous, mysterious ability to fly.

For some people it is enough just to see a bird and observe its actions. Others want to identify the bird, learn about its lifestyle and behavior. Name That Bird encourages both.

With more than 800 species of birds in North America, it's easy to feel overwhelmed trying to identify the birds that grace your backyard feeders. But it is just this diversity that fascinates us all and keeps us wanting more. With this book you will begin to understand the disparities between the different species—their distinctive behavior and habitats, their color and markings, their varied palates—and quickly discover the mystery behind these beautiful, vibrant creatures.

About This Book

Name That Bird doesn't attempt to show every visitor north of the Mexican border. Instead, this book focuses on the ones you are most likely to see. Maps accompany each bird, indicating migration, breeding, and wintering ranges. But remember, birds sometimes stray from their usual range, and changes in range are inevitable over time, so you just may be surprised one day to see a bird that's in the "wrong" place at the "wrong" time. Separated into three different sections, from perching birds to hummingbirds and other backyard guests, such as the cuckoo, roadrunner, and owl, Name That Bird makes it easy to find out who is pecking at your back door by focusing on size, color and markings, behavior, and habitat. More than 30 Feathered Facts sprinkled throughout provide insight into the unique ways these winged wonders court, nest, socialize, find food, or simply spend their day.

GETTING STARTED

Beginning and intermediate birders need little equipment. This field guide, a pair of binoculars, and a notebook for recording your sightings are all you really need (see "Quick Tips for First-Time Birders," page 10). Most birds are active

Quick Tips for First-Time Birders

- Keep this book handy.

- Invest in a pair of binoculars. The most popular sizes are 7 x 35 and 8 x 40.

- Get familiar with the birds in your area. There are checklists of birds for every state. Check online or with your state park.

- Know the birds' habitats—are they ground-foraging birds or do they prefer perching on a high branch?

- Get involved with some bird groups. Call your local Audubon Society or nature center. Your parks commission may also offer some events.

- Attract your favorites to your backyard. For instance, if hummingbirds are your favorite, hang a nectar feeder (see pages 106–107); if you marvel at the bright red plumage of the northern cardinal, hang a hopper feeder filled with nuts and berries.

- Keep a diary to record your bird sightings. This could be a mere list of species seen or a notebook filled with extensive notes.

from dawn to midmorning, so to maximize your sightings, rise early, grab a steaming cup of coffee or tea, and quietly head out your back door when nature is in full swing. Look for the following characteristics to help identify your backyard visitors:

Body size and shape: Pick one bird as your starting point for size. Most people are familiar with the American robin. This is considered a medium-sized bird, at 9 to 11 inches in length. Is your bird smaller, like the black-capped chickadee? Or is it larger, like the blue jay or crow? Also note the shape of the bird. Is it slender, like a mourning dove or swallow? Or is it more robust, like the northern cardinal?

Color and markings: These are the attributes that most tellingly reveal a bird's identity, even though you may not be able to accurately see everything you wish before your subject flies off. With more experience you will be able to quickly spot the significant details that separate a closely related species—for instance, the white stripes on the wings, the red belly, the black head, or the eye ring. These flashes of color are called field marks. (See "Birds with Prominent Yellow Markings," page 27.)

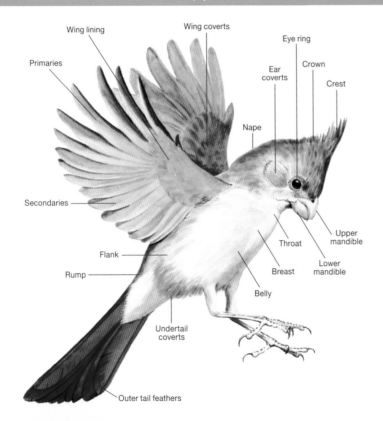

Wing lining

Wing coverts

Eye ring

Primaries

Ear coverts

Crown

Crest

Nape

Secondaries

Upper mandible

Throat

Flank

Lower mandible

Rump

Breast

Belly

Undertail coverts

Outer tail feathers

Habitat symbols
The icons below indicate where these birds are predominantly found.

urban/suburban

forest

grassland/meadow/brush

saltwater

freshwater

desert

breeding

migration

all year

winter

Idento-checks call your attention to certain features mentioned in the "What to Look for" identification capsules.

behavior. For example, woodpeckers have a rigid, powerful, chisel-shaped beak so they can bore into wood to find insects; cardinals and finches have short, thick conical beaks to help crack seeds and nuts; and the hummingbird's long, slender beak allows it to sip nectar.

Tail: Another way to differentiate a species is by their tail. Is it short and wide, like the cedar waxwing? Long and narrow, like the black-capped chickadee? Is it forked, like the scissor-tailed flycatcher? Does it stick straight up, like the wrentit's?

Behavior: Once you start observing your backyard visitors, you will notice that not only are their food-gathering techniques different from one another—some perch at feeders, while others forage on the ground—you will notice that the species themselves have distinct personalities. Jays are bold and comfortable around humans; mockingbirds are territorial bullies; and chickadees and titmice are delightful little performers. The Feathered Facts throughout this book will provide insight into some of the distinctive traits that make birds so delightful to watch.

Beak: Classifying birds according to the shape of their beak is an excellent way to narrow your choices, because there are so many different types. Sharp and conical, tiny and narrow, hooked, or daggerlike, just to name a few. Interestingly enough, the shape of the beak also indicates the type of food a bird eats and therefore provides clues to

The Great Backyard Bird Count

For four days each year in February, just before the spring migrations begin, people of all ages across America gather in parks, woodlands, backyards, wetlands, and elsewhere to participate in the Great Backyard Bird Count.

This joint project of the Cornell Laboratory of Ornithology and the National Audubon Society, together with their Canadian partner, Bird Studies Canada, is an effort to create a real-time snapshot of where the birds are across the continent and how they are surviving the winter. The data gathered from the participants help scientists to:

- observe how snow and temperature influence the bird population.
- explore the diversity of birds in rural versus urban areas.
- compare the timing of migrations with past years.
- see if bird diseases, such as the West Nile Virus, are affecting the bird count.
- find out if any birds are undergoing a worrisome decline that would entail conservationists to take action.

Participants can contribute as little as 15 minutes on any one day or count for as long as they prefer, every day of the event. After gathering their data and tallying the highest number of birds of each species seen at one time, participants submit their counts online at the Great Backyard Bird Count website (www.gbbc.birdsource.org).

In 2010 the birds most frequently seen during the Great Backyard Bird Count were:

northern cardinal	53,513
dark-eyed junco	48,700
mourning dove	45,557
downy woodpecker	39,668
blue jay	39,484
American goldfinch	38,190
tufted titmouse	36,101
house finch	33,068
American crow	30,649
black-capped chickadee	29,823

The top 5 states submitting counts were New York, California, Ohio, North Carolina, and Pennsylvania.

Source: www.gbbc.birdsource.org

perching birds

The undulating flight of the finch, the acrobatic artistry of the bushtit, the melodious song of the chickadee, the unwavering loyalty of the cardinal, the remarkable intelligence of the crow, the frenzied courtship of the meadowlark....These are the perchers, also known as the passerines.

The largest and most unique family of birds, perchers make up more than half of all the birds in the world. Because of this, there is great diversity among them; tails, bills, color, wingspan, size, shape, and behavior all vary dramatically from one to the next. But there is one characteristic they all have in common: All passerines have three toes that point forward and one that points backward, all joining the foot at the same level, enabling them to rest on branches, telephone wires, fenceposts, grasses, feeders, and anywhere else they decide to roost, allowing us to observe them in all sorts of wonderful and exciting places.

cardinals, buntings, and tanagers

These colorful medium-sized songbirds have heavy seed-crushing bills and socialize in either pairs or small clusters. Most are territorial. During migration the male arrives before the female and defends the territory against other males. Courting, pairing, nesting, and raising young also occur within these borders.

Northern Cardinal *Cardinalis cardinalis*

Length: 7–8 ½ in.

What to look for: prominent crest; conical reddish bill; male bright red, with black around eye and bill; female brownish yellow, with red on wings and tail.

Habitat: open woods, forest edges, thickets, suburbs, parks.

The cardinal's rich coloring and its readiness to come to feeders have made it a favorite among birdwatchers. Its varied musical repertoire consists of loud, clear whistles that are usually repeated several times—*wheet, wheet, wheet, wheet, chew, chew, chew, cheedle, cheedle, cheedle.* Male and female may sing alternately, as if in response to each other. Cardinals also have a metallic *pink* note. This species is one of a number of southern birds that have extended their ranges northward during this century. Among the others are the mockingbird, tufted titmouse, and red-bellied woodpecker.

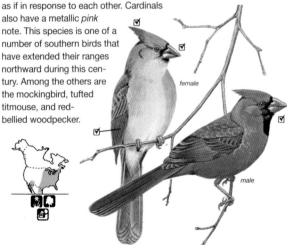

female

male

male

female

Painted Bunting
Passerina ciris

Length: 5–5½ in.

What to look for: male with blue head, red underparts and rump, and green back; female green above, yellowish below.

Habitat: brushy fields, forest edges, shrubby streamsides, fencerows, towns.

Considered by many to be North America's most beautifully colored bird, the male painted bunting justly merits the nickname "nonpareil" (unequaled). Males are very conspicuous as they sing from high, exposed perches, but the species favors thick ground cover and shrubbery for feeding and nesting. The majority of painted buntings migrate to Central America, though some may overwinter in Florida.

Lark Bunting *Calamospiza melanocorys*

Length: 5½–7 in.

What to look for: male black or dark gray, with large white wing patch; female, immature, and winter male brown above, finely streaked below, with light wing patch.

Habitat: prairies, semiarid areas, brushy fields.

Lark buntings are gregarious. They winter and travel in flocks and nest fairly close together. The conspicuously marked breeding males perform song flights in which they rise more or less straight up to a height of 10 to 30 feet and then rock slowly down with stiff wings, butterfly-fashion, singing from start to landing. Often several will do this together.

male

female

Choosing Seed for Your Backyard Visitors

The indigo bunting is a seed-eating bird, as are cardinals, grosbeaks, sparrows, and finches. It's easy to tell by their short conical bill, which is great for crushing seeds and nuts. The most popular seeds are sunflower, safflower, sunflower hearts, niger seed, millet, corn, and nut meats.

The following are some guidelines when buying and storing seeds:

- Some commercial seed mixes are filled with inexpensive seed that gets tossed out of the feeder because birds don't like it. To cut down on waste, purchase individual varieties and make your own mix.

- Sunflower seed attracts the largest variety of birds. The black-oil sunflower seed contains a kernel with a very high fat content, which is ideal for most winter birds.

- Try not to buy seed that is dusty or moldy or sticks together in clumps. Those are good indicators that the seed is old.

- To add some extra flavor to your seed, throw in some cranberries, peanuts, or raisins. Birds also need some grit in their diet to help their digestion, so be sure to include some ground-up eggshells or sand.

- For leftovers, store seed away from the house in an airtight container so that insects and mice don't find their way into the bag.

female

Feathered fact
What this songster lacks in quality is made up in persistence, singing well into the late summer, when most birds have long since fallen silent.

male

Indigo Bunting *Passerina cyanea*

Length: 4½–5½ in.

What to look for: male indigo-blue, with blackish wings and tail, no wingbars; female brown above, whitish below, with faint streaking on breast.

Habitat: brushy areas, scrubby fields, forest edges.

The male indigo bunting is one of the few birds giving full-voiced performances at midday. A typical song has been written down as *sir, chewe, chewe, cheer, cheer, swe, swe, chir, chir, chir, sir, sir, see, see, fish, fish, fish.* The western lazuli bunting (Passerina amoena), with sky-blue head, rusty breast, and wingbars, interbreeds with the indigo where their ranges overlap.

Snow Bunting *Plectrophenax nivalis*

Length: 5½–7 in.

What to look for: mostly white; breeding male with black on back, wings, and tail; nonbreeding male with reddish brown on head and shoulders; female paler.

Habitat: tundra; prairies, meadows, beaches (migration, winter).

The snowflakes or snow birds breed farther north than any other species of songbird. The males arrive on their arctic breeding grounds by mid-May, three or four weeks earlier than the females. The Eskimos welcome them as harbingers of spring. Snow buntings nest mainly on rocky terrain, usually building their bulky fur- and feather-lined nests in holes and crannies. In winter they flock along coasts and in open country. They feed on fallen grain in fields and pastures and on weed seeds, as well as on sand fleas and other insects.

breeding male

nonbreeding male

female

male

Scarlet Tanager
Piranga olivacea

Length: 6–7 in.

What to look for: male scarlet, with black wings and tail (in fall, red replaced by yellowish green); female yellowish green, with darker wings and tail.

Habitat: thick deciduous woodlands, suburbs, parks.

The scarlet tanager's song is not hard to pick out: Listen to a robin sing for a while, then listen for the same song with a burr in it. The species also has a distinctive, hoarse call— *chick-kurr* in the East, sometimes *chip-chiree* elsewhere. Scarlet tanagers devour many destructive caterpillars and wood-boring beetles, most often but not exclusively in oaks. Young males may be principally orange or splotched with red and yellow.

female

male

Summer Tanager
Piranga rubra

Length: 6–7½ in.

What to look for: yellowish bill; male red; female yellowish green above, yellow below.

Habitat: woodlands; in uplands, drier forests of oak, hickory, or pine.

Tanagers are mainly insect eaters, though they do take some buds and fruits. The summer tanager is especially fond of beetles and bees, and it will tear wasps' nests apart to get at the larvae. The hard parts of beetles are not digested but are coughed up as pellets. This species builds a flimsy nest on a horizontal bough. Its song is a more musical version of the scarlet tanager's, and its spluttery call is traditionally written as *chicky-tucky-tuck.* A less common species, similar in appearance but with a dark mask, is the hepatic tanager (*Piranga flava*) of the mountainous Southwest.

Western Tanager *Piranga ludoviciana*

Length: 6–7 in.

What to look for: male bright yellow, with red head and black on upper back, wings, and tail (no red on nonbreeder); female greenish above, yellowish below (only female tanager with wingbars).

Habitat: open mixed and coniferous woodlands; other forests (migration).

The song of the western tanager is much the same as that of the scarlet tanager—a series of short phrases separated by pauses. Its call is two- or three-syllabled—*pit-ic, pit-it-ic.* On migration, flocks of western tanagers pass through valleys, plains, and foothills. They nest mostly in the mountains, in firs and pines, often at high elevations. Like other tanagers, they lay three to five eggs. The female alone incubates, but both parents share the care and feeding of the nestlings.

female

male

warblers

There are a great number of perching birds known as warblers, but they are not all closely related. What they do have in common, however, is their love of insects. These small, colorful, vocal birds flock in large mixes—usually six or more species—during the spring and fall migrations. The sound of dripping water is one of the best ways to attract these active birds.

female

male

Feathered fact
Latin Americans call these busy little birds candelitas, because they dance like little candle flames scouring blossoms, twigs, and leaves for insects.

American Redstart *Setophaga ruticilla*

Length: 4–5½ in.

What to look for: male black, with white belly and orangish patches on wings and tail; female and immature grayish above, white below, with yellow patches.

Habitat: second-growth deciduous forests, thickets, suburbs, parks.

One of the most common warblers, this is also one of the most attractive. Flashes of color on the fanned-out wings and tail ("red-start" means "red-tailed") make the lively birds resemble flitting butterflies as they catch insects on the wing. The variable song is a set of single or double notes on one pitch, which may end with a higher or lower note—*zee-zee-zee-zee-zee-zeeo*.

Tennessee Warbler
Vermivora peregrina

Length: 4–5 in.

What to look for: gray cap; white eye stripe; greenish above, white below; female and immature yellowish.

Habitat: open mixed and deciduous forests, brushy areas, forest edges.

The ornithologist Alexander Wilson discovered this species and the related Nashville warbler *(Vermivora ruficapilla)* on an 1810 bird-finding trip in the South. Like many birds, these two were named for the places where they were first seen.

Prothonotary Warbler
Protonotaria citrea

Length: 4 ½–5 in.

What to look for: bright orange-yellow head and breast, fading to lighter below; gray wings and tail; female more yellowish.

Habitat: wooded bottomlands; lowland swamps; moist, frequently flooded woods.

Court officers, or prothonotaries, who sometimes wore bright yellow robes inspired the name of this handsome species. The prothonotary warbler is a bird of wooded swamps and riverbanks. As a rule, it nests in a tree cavity or a deserted woodpecker hole, but in some localities it is tame enough to choose a birdhouse or any other small container.

Northern Parula *Parula americana*

Length: 3½–4 in.

What to look for: blue above, with greenish yellow patch on back; white wingbars; throat and breast yellow; darker band across throat (male).

Habitat: humid forests, usually near water; other forests (migration).

The name parula means "little titmouse," a reference to the bird's active behavior as it forages through the foliage for insects. In the South the parula hollows out a shallow nest in trailing clumps of Spanish Moss; in northern forests it nests in Usnea lichen. Its song is a buzzy trill, sliding upward in pitch and snapping off at the end—*zzzzzzzz-zup.*

Black-and-White Warbler
Mniotilta varia

Length: 4–5½ in.

What to look for: streaked black and white above, white below; white stripe through crown; female and immature duller.

Habitat: forests.

Early ornithologists called this species the black-and-white creeper or creeping warbler. Constantly in motion, it searches for insects on bark, moving along head up like a creeper or down like a nuthatch. It has a brisk, sibilant song, usually a string of high-pitched double syllables—*weesee, weesee, weesee, weesee.*

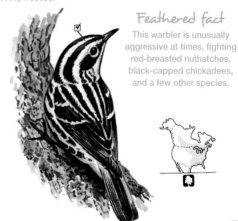

Feathered fact

This warbler is unusually aggressive at times, fighting red-breasted nuthatches, black-capped chickadees, and a few other species.

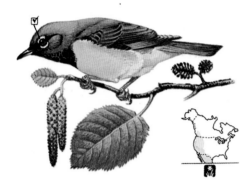

MacGillivray's Warbler
Oporornis tolmiei

Length: 4½–5½ in.

What to look for: slate-gray head, blackish near breast; incomplete white eye ring; olive-green above, yellow below; female and immature duller.

Habitat: dense brushy areas, moist thickets.

Three warblers have gray hoods—this one, the similar mourning warbler *(Oporornis philadelphia)* of the North and East, and the Connecticut warbler *(Oporornis agilis),* also a northern bird. All three skulk in dense vegetation near the ground. This species was named for a Scottish ornithologist who edited Audubon's writings.

Northern Waterthrush
Seiurus noveboracensis

Length: 5–6 in.

What to look for: pale eye stripe; dark brown above, buffy with dark streaks below; teeters continually.

Habitat: wet woodlands; brushy areas (migration).

Look and listen for this warbler near placid water. The closely related Louisiana waterthrush *(Seiurus motacilla)* is more likely near fast-flowing streams. Both species bob and teeter along over banks, rocks, and logs. Their looks are similar, but with practice they can be distinguished by their voices. Both build their nests, of moss and other bits of vegetation, near water.

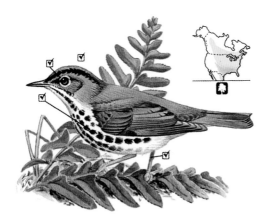

Ovenbird *Seiurus aurocapillus*

Length: 5–6 in.

What to look for: olive above, with orange crown bordered by black; white below, with dark streaks; white eye ring; pinkish legs; walks on ground.

Habitat: deciduous woodlands.

Once it is familiar, the voice of the ovenbird is one of the most obvious in the woods. The song begins softly and builds to a ringing crescendo—*teacher, teacher, teacher, teacher!* The Ovenbird is a ground-dwelling warbler. Its covered nest, which accounts for its name, is generally hidden on the forest floor.

Hooded Warbler *Wilsonia citrina*

Length: 4¼–5½ in.

What to look for: male with yellow face, black hood, black throat; female with brownish cap; greenish above, yellow below; white on tail.

Habitat: dense deciduous forests, wooded swamps, thickets; usually near water.

In the East two common warblers have black caps on yellow heads. One is this species; the other is Wilson's warbler *(Wilsonia pusilla),* which ranges the continent and lacks the hooded's black bib. The hooded warbler is a bird of the undergrowth, nesting low in a bush or sapling. From the outside the nest looks like a wad of dead leaves, but inside it is an impressive construction of bark, plant fibers, down, grass, and spiderweb.

Feathered fact

Male hooded warblers catch flying insects, while the female hunts closer to the ground.

Canada Warbler
Wilsonia canadensis

Length: 4½–5½ in.

What to look for: gray above, yellow below; "spectacles"; male with black "necklace"; female duller, with faint "necklace."

Habitat: mature deciduous woodlands near streams or swamps; moist brushy areas; second-growth forests (migration).

This distinctively marked species breeds in cool, damp forests in Canada and elsewhere. It is usually a ground-nester, frequently choosing a site in or near a moss-covered log or stump. Its song is a bright, rapid warble on one pitch.

Common Yellowthroat
Geothlypis trichas

Length: 4–5½ in.

What to look for: male with black mask, edged above with white; greenish brown above, with yellow throat, upper breast, and undertail; female without mask.

Habitat: wet brushy areas, freshwater and saltwater marshes.

This familiar warbler, black-masked like a little bandit, is usually first seen peering at the intruder from the depths of a shrub or thicket. Sooner or later the yellowthroat announces itself with a rhythmic *witchery, witchery, witchery* or variations on that theme. Yellowthroats sometimes nest in loose colonies, but most often breeding pairs are well distributed through brushy or marshy areas.

male

female

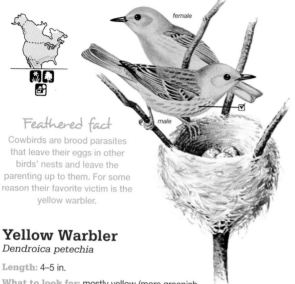

female

male

Feathered fact

Cowbirds are brood parasites that leave their eggs in other birds' nests and leave the parenting up to them. For some reason their favorite victim is the yellow warbler.

Yellow Warbler

Dendroica petechia

Length: 4–5 in.

What to look for: mostly yellow (more greenish above); male streaked with reddish on breast; female duller.

Habitat: riverside woodlands, wet thickets, brushy marsh edges, orchards, suburbs, parks.

This species has the largest breeding range of any warbler and is common not only in most of North America but as far south as Peru. The yellow warbler often nests in willows, alders, or other shrubs along the edge of a swamp or road; its neat cup of silvery plant fibers is usually built in a low fork. The male is a persistent singer with two basic songs: *pip-pip-pip-sissewa-is sweet* and *wee-see-wee-see-wiss-wiss-u*.

Birds with Prominent Yellow Markings

The yellow warbler and prothonotary warbler (inset) are easy to spot because of their extensive markings. The following are some others that are known for their bright yellow plumage. All of these can be found in this book (see "Index of Birds Profiled in This Book," pages 118 and 119).

- verdin
- northern parula
- MacGillivray's warbler
- American redstart
- Canada warbler
- hooded warbler
- common yellowthroat
- magnolia warbler
- yellow-rumped warbler
- palm warbler
- black-throated green warbler
- yellow-throated warbler
- blackburnian warbler
- pine warbler
- American goldfinch
- northern flicker
- western kingbird
- great crested flycatcher
- horned lark
- yellow-breasted chat
- western meadowlark
- yellow-headed blackbird
- Scott's oriole
- evening grosbeak

Yellow-breasted Chat *Icteria virens*

Length: 6½–7½ in.

What to look for: largest warbler; dark mask; heavy bill; white "spectacles"; green above; yellow breast.

Habitat: dense thickets and tangles, usually near water; shrubby areas in upland pastures.

For years ornithologists have been saying that this bird is in all probability not really a warbler. It is half again as big as some species and much more robust. Its song is loud and varied. One observer who tried to put a passage into syllables got this result: "*C-r-r-r-r-r—whirr—that's it—chee—quack, cluck—yit-yit-yit—now hit it—tr-r-r—when—caw, caw—cut, cut—tea-boy— who, who—mew, mew—and so on till you are tired of listening.*"

Magnolia Warbler *Dendroica magnolia*

Length: 4–5 in.

What to look for: black above, yellow streaked with black below; gray cap; yellow rump; wings and tail black, with large white patches; female and immature paler.

Habitat: coniferous forests; other wooded areas (migration).

Alexander Wilson first sighted this warbler in magnolia trees, and the scientific name he gave it included the word magnolia. Eventually "magnolia warbler," being a pretty way of referring to a beautiful bird, became the common name. But as one authority remarked, if the warbler had to be named after a tree, spruce or balsam would have been more appropriate for this northern forest bird.

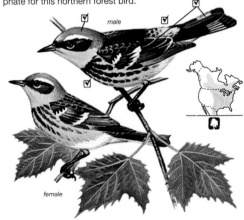

male

female

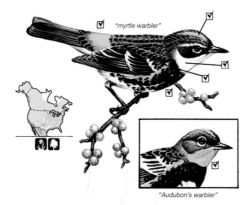

"myrtle warbler"

"Audubon's warbler"

Yellow-rumped Warbler
Dendroica coronata

Length: 4½–5½ in.

What to look for: male with yellow crown, rump, and shoulder patch, white (East) or yellow (West) throat, black bib, white tail patches (visible mainly in flight); female and immature paler, browner.

Habitat: coniferous and mixed forests; other woodlands, thickets (migration, winter).

This is one of the most abundant of our warblers, and at times in migration it seems to outnumber all the others combined. It has a bright, loud chip call that is easily learned, but recognizing its trilling song takes practice. Audubon's warbler (the western subspecies) and the eastern myrtle were long considered separate species.

Palm Warbler *Dendroica palmarum*

Length: 4–5½ in.

What to look for: reddish cap (breeding); underparts yellow or whitish, streaked, with yellow undertail; wags tail.

Habitat: forest swamps, bogs; brushy areas (migration, winter).

Ornithologists first observed this warbler wintering among the palms of Florida; hence, its common name—surely a misnomer for a species breeding in northern bogs. During migration the palm qarbler is often seen on the ground or in a low tree, where it flicks its tail up and down. The prairie warbler *(Dendroica discolor),* common in areas crossed by migrating palms, flicks its tail from side to side. It lacks the red cap and yellow undertail.

Black-throated Gray Warbler
Dendroica nigrescens

Length: 4–5 in.

What to look for: male with black head and throat, white stripe above and below eye; gray above, white below; female and immature paler, with less black.

Habitat: oak, juniper, and pinyon forests, mixed woodlands with heavy undergrowth.

Like a number of other *Dendroica* warblers, this species is partial to evergreen trees, at least in the mountains of the Northwest. Farther south it breeds in the dry, scrubby growth of canyon and valley walls. Its nests are not easy to find; they are often located, for example, at the junction of several leafy twigs that hold and screen the structure.

Black-throated Green Warbler
Dendroica virens

Length: 4–5 in.

What to look for: yellow face; black throat and breast; green above; white wingbars; female and immature duller, with less black.

Habitat: coniferous forests; other woodlands (migration, winter).

The black-throated green has a preference for pines and other conifers, but during migration it can be seen high up in a deciduous tree or low down in a roadside thicket. This is the only eastern warbler with yellowish cheeks. Other handsome, similar-looking species are townsend's warbler *(Dendroica townsendi)* and the hermit warbler *(Dendroica occidentalis),* both of the Far West.

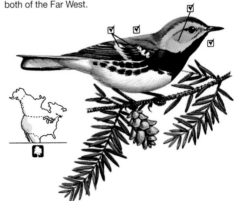

Yellow-throated Warbler
Dendroica dominica

Length: 5–5½ in.

What to look for: yellow throat; gray above; black-and-white pattern on face; female similar but duller.

Habitat: pine and oak forests, cypress swamps.

The song of the yellow-throated warbler is a clear, bright whistle—*see-wee, see-wee, see-wee, swee, swee, swee, swee*—that speeds up and drops in pitch toward the end. This bird seems less nervous than many other warblers. It forages carefully for insects on tree bark in much the manner as the brown creeper or the black-and-white warbler.

Black-throated Blue Warbler
Dendroica caerulescens

Length: 5–5½ in.

What to look for: male dark blue above, with prominent white wing spot and black face, throat, and sides; female dull olive (paler below), with white wing spot.

Habitat: deciduous and mixed forests with heavy undergrowth.

The male black-throated blue looks the same in spring, summer, and fall, so it is one of the easiest warblers to recognize. It is easy to spot, too, for it is usually found quite low—in rhododendron, laurel, and similar undergrowth. Observing another blue-backed species, the cerulean warbler *(Dendroica cerulea),* may require a lot of neck-craning, since it usually feeds high in a tree.

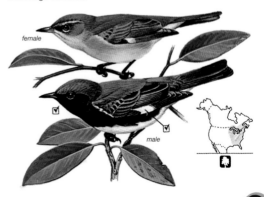

female

male

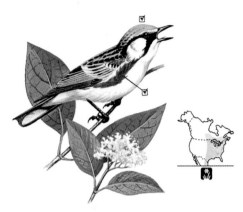

Chestnut-sided Warbler
Dendroica pensylvanica

Length: 4–5 in.

What to look for: male with yellow cap and chestnut sides, whitish below; female duller, with spotty chestnut areas; immature yellowish green above, white below.

Habitat: brushy fields, open woodlands, farmlands.

The distinctive song of the chestnut-sided warbler helps to locate the bird. The usual version approximates *tsee, see, see, see, see, swee-BEAT-chew,* with the last note dropping in pitch; several generations of birders have used the words "I wish to see Miss Beecher" as a memory aid. The bay-breasted warbler *(Dendroica castanea)* is more richly colored, with deep chestnut on head, breast, and sides.

Blackburnian Warbler
Dendroica fusca

Length: 4–5 ½ in.

What to look for: male with bright orange throat, striped black back, broad white wingbars; female and immature paler, brownish; facial pattern always present.

Habitat: coniferous or mixed forests; other woodlands (migration).

A bird of the deep woods, the blackburnian nests in a variety of conifers—spruces, firs, pines, hemlocks. On migration it is a treetop forager and singer, often difficult to spot despite the glowing orange throat. Its song is thin and buzzy, ending with a single high, up-sliding note. The species was named for Anna Blackburn, an 18th-century patron of ornithology.

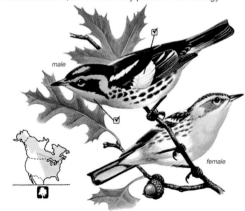

male

female

Pine Warbler
Dendroica pinus

Length: 5–5½ in.

What to look for: olive-green above, yellowish with streaks below; white wingbars; female duller.

Habitat: open pine forests; deciduous woodlands (migration).

The name of this bird is quite appropriate: Except when on migration, the pine warbler "sticks to pine woods as a cocklebur sticks to a dog's tail." The nest is usually built in a clump of pine needles or on the top of a pine bough between 15 and 80 feet from the ground. The song is a loose, sweet trill.

Feathered fact

Except during spring and fall migrations, these little birds are rarely spotted too far away from their favorite pine trees, such as pitch, jack, white, Norway, and scrub.

Blackpoll Warbler *Dendroica striata*

Length: 4¼–5½ in.

What to look for: male with black cap, white face, black-streaked flanks; female browner, without cap; in fall both sexes greenish, with white wingbars.

Habitat: coniferous woodlands; other woodlands (migration).

Many birders greet the blackpolls' arrival each spring with some regret, for it signals the end of the exciting warbler migration. The blackpoll's song is said to be the highest in pitch of any songbird's (some people can't hear it at all). It is a fast series of single syllables more or less on the same thin note, loudest in the middle.

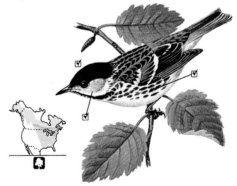

mockingbirds, thrashers, and thrushes

All three of these feathered gems are recognized for their long tails and long, curved bills; excellent song; and ability to mimic other birds. But far more melodious, the mockingbird has been hailed as the King of Song. It can imitate more than 30 birdsongs in rapid succession, along with other sounds, such as squeaky hinges, barking dogs, and chirping crickets.

Northern Mockingbird *Mimus polyglottos*

Length: 9–11 in.

What to look for: gray above, whitish below; tail long, blackish; white wing patches; no black eye mask.

Habitat: open areas, farmland, suburbs, parks; scrubby growth near water (dry areas).

Within its range the mockingbird is much more common than the similarly colored shrikes. It is best known for its song, which may be heard day or night. Typically the bird repeats a phrase over and over (perhaps half a dozen times), then drops that phrase and goes on to another. Often the phrases are imitations of other birds' songs, and "mockers" have also been known to sound like frogs, crickets, and dogs, among others. They do not need a recent reminder, it seems, but can remember phrases for several months, at least.

Gray Catbird
Dumetella carolinensis

Length: 7–9 in.

What to look for: long tail; dark gray, with black cap and rusty undertail.

Habitat: undergrowth in woodlands, hedgerows, brushy areas, suburbs, parks.

Often in the nesting season this trim bird is a close neighbor of man. Like the mockingbird, the gray catbird is regarded as a mimic, but it is less an actual imitator than a plagiarist of musical ideas. As one listener put it, the catbird "suggests the songs of various birds—never delivers the notes in their way!" It burbles along, now loud, now soft, uttering a long run of squeaky phrases, seldom repeating itself. It gets its name from its call note—a petulant, catlike mew.

Feathered fact

The male sings with a cacophony of shrieks, squeaks, and whistles, as well as the cat's *m-e-e-e-o-w* from which the species derives its name.

Brown Thrasher
Toxostoma rufum

Length: 9½–11 in.

What to look for: long tail; bright reddish brown above; two white wingbars; white below, streaked with brown.

Habitat: open brushy areas, forest edges, hedgerows, thickets, suburbs, parks.

Thrashers, like mockingbirds and catbirds, are members of the family *Mimidae,* or mimic thrushes. (The name thrasher derives from the word thrush.) A characteristic of this group is the imitation of sounds. The most notable quality of the thrasher's music, aside from the occasional imitation, is the phrasing. The loud, ringing song has been written in this vein: *"Hurry up, hurry up; plow it, plow it; harrow it; chuck; sow it, sow it, sow it; chuck-chuck, chuck-chuck; hoe it, hoc it."* The bird is usually seen singing from a high perch out in the open.

mockingbirds, thrashers, and thrushes

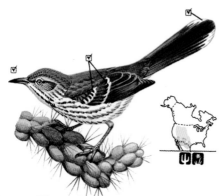

Sage Thrasher *Oreoscoptes montanus*

Length: 8–9 in.

What to look for: small thrasher; bill short, thin; gray-brown above, with 2 white wingbars; white below, streaked with brown; tail tipped with white.

Habitat: shrubby areas, brushy slopes, sagebrush; deserts (winter).

This small thrasher is a bird of the dry foothills and plains. It nests on the ground or, more usually, low down in sagebrush or other shrubby growth. Nest materials include twigs, plant stems, and bark fibers, with hair and fine roots for lining. Occasionally sage thrashers build a twig "awning" in the branches above the nest, as if to provide shade from the hot sun. Their song, a series of trills and warbles somewhat like that of the eastern brown thrasher, sounds more fluent because it lacks the pauses between the repeated phrases.

California Thrasher
Toxostoma redivivum

Length: 11–13 in.

What to look for: bill long, curved down; long tail; dark gray-brown above, lighter below; cinnamon belly and undertail; dark mustache; light eye stripe.

Habitat: dry brushy areas, suburbs, parks.

Many birds that feed on the ground forage by scratching with their feet, kicking over leaves and other debris. But the California thrasher uses its long, curved bill, uncovering hidden food and chopping deep into the earth after buried larvae. Its diet includes beetles, ants, bees, and caterpillars. Very strong afoot, this thrasher seems to prefer running to flying except in emergencies. Not all grayish sickle-billed thrashers are necessarily this species. Three other somewhat similar thrashers are found in California and the Southwest: the curve-billed (*Toxostoma curvirostre*), Le Conte's (*Toxostoma lecontei*), and the crissal (*Toxostoma dorsale*).

immature

American Robin *Turdus migratorius*

Length: 9–11 in.

What to look for: bright reddish orange below; dark gray above (head paler on female), with broken eye ring and white-tipped tail; immature with light, speckled breast.

Habitat: open forests, farmlands, suburbs, parks; sheltered areas with fruit on trees (winter).

The robin, a member of the thrush family, is one of the most neighborly of birds. A pair will often build their nest—a neat cup of mud and grasses—on a branch of a dooryard tree or on the ledge of a porch, and they hunt confidently for earthworms on the lawn and in the garden, regardless of human activities nearby. Robins eat insects as well as worms; they also like fruits, both wild and cultivated.

Best Plants for Berry Eaters

Robins love fruit, and so do mockingbirds, waxwings, woodpeckers, orioles, tanagers, and chickadees. The number of shrubs, vines, and small trees that produce fruit that birds will eat is extensive. These 14 are a good place to start.

1 **barberry**
   Berberis species, Zones 3 to 8

2 **chokecherry**
   Prunus virginiana, Zones 2 to 8

3 **crabapple**
   Malus species, Zones 3 to 8

4 **highbush cranberry**
   Viburnum trilobum, Zones 2 to 7

5 **manzanita**
   Arctostaphylos species, Zones 8 to 10

6 **mountain ash**
   Sorbus species, Zones 2 to 7

7 **mulberry**
   Morus species, Zones 4 to 8

8 **pagoda dogwood**
   Cornus alternifolia, Zones 3 to 7

9 **serviceberry**
   Amelanchier species, Zones 2 to 9

10 **spicebush**
   Lindera bezoin, Zones 4 to 9

11 **sweetbay**
   Magnolia virginiana, Zones 5 to 9

12 **virginia creeper**
   Parthenocissus quinquefolia, Zones 3 to 9

13 **washington hawthorn**
   Crataegus phaenopyrum, Zones 3 to 8

14 **winterberry**
   Ilex verticillata, Zones 3 to 9

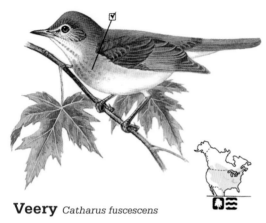

Veery *Catharus fuscescens*

Length: 6½–7½ in.

What to look for: brownish red above; whitish below, with buffy, brown-spotted breast band; in West, darker and less reddish.

Habitat: humid deciduous woodlands, river groves, wooded swamps.

The name veery is said to have been coined in imitation of the bird's song, a downward-spiraling series of hollow, liquid phrases best written as *whree-u, whree-u, whree-u*, and so on. Many thrushes—this one in particular—sing far into the dusk and sometimes even after dark. Veeries feed on the ground, hopping along and turning over dead leaves.

Varied Thrush *Ixoreus naevius*

Length: 8–9½ in.

What to look for: dark gray above, with pale orange eye stripe and wingbars; orange below, with black breast band; female paler, browner, with gray breast band.

Habitat: damp coniferous and mixed forests, other moist woodlands, wooded canyons.

The varied thrush, though a native of the Pacific Northwest, is famous as a winter wanderer outside its normal range. The species has turned up in many unexpected places, frequently as far east as the Atlantic Coast. Even for a thrush, its song is remarkable. The singer makes use of a "scale" of five or six notes and—choosing these pitches in no particular order—whistles a series of pure single notes, each note rising to a crescendo and then fading away to a brief pause.

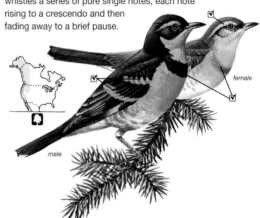

female

male

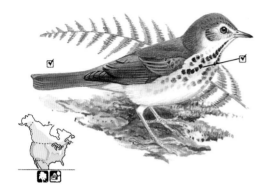

Hermit Thrush *Catharus guttatus*

Length: 6–7½ in.

What to look for: brown above, with reddish rump and tail; white below, with dark spots on throat and breast.

Habitat: moist coniferous or mixed forests; other woodlands, parks (migration).

The song of this retiring bird is an extraordinary sequence of phrases on varying pitches. Each phrase begins with a single whistle and closes with a jumble of brilliant, bubbly notes. On nesting territory in the northern forests, its song may often be heard with the songs of Swainson's and the gray-cheeked thrush (*Catharus ustulatus* and *minimus*), olive-backed birds that lack the hermit's rusty tail.

Wood Thrush *Hylocichla mustelina*

Length: 7½–8½ in.

What to look for: head and upper back reddish brown; white below, with large, dark brown spots from throat to belly.

Habitat: moist deciduous forests, suburbs, parks.

This thrush nests in dark, damp woods, where it builds a tidy cup of grasses, stems, and dead leaves, usually mixed with mud and lined with roots. Often strips of birch bark, paper, or white cloth are woven into the structure. The wood thrush's song is complex and beautiful—a series of brief, liquid phrases often interspersed with a high trill.

Feathered fact
Within minutes of her young's hatching, a mother wood thrush may start to clear away the shell.

male

female

Eastern Bluebird
Sialia sialis

Length: 5–7 in.

What to look for: male bright blue above, with orange-red throat and breast; female paler; immature mostly gray, spotted with white on back and breast.

Habitat: open areas with scattered trees and fencerows; farmlands, orchards, suburbs.

The sweet chirrup and the flash of blue in garden or orchard or along a rural road have made the eastern bluebird a special favorite. But for many years this much-admired bird has been in trouble: introduced house sparrows and Starlings have taken over its preferred tree holes. Fortunately, bluebirds will nest in birdhouses specially designed to keep out the alien intruders. In many areas hundreds of these houses have been set up along "bluebird trails"—ambitious projects that have halted the species' decline and even reversed it in some places.

Mountain Bluebird
Sialia currucoides

Length: 6–7 ½ in.

What to look for: male sky-blue above, light blue below; female mostly gray, with some blue; immature grayer, with streaked underparts.

Habitat: open high-elevation areas with scattered trees and brush; sometimes in lowlands.

Both the eastern and the western bluebird *(Sialia mexicana)* hunt for insects by scanning the ground from perches on wires or fenceposts and then dropping on the prey. The mountain bluebird, which eats a greater proportion of insects than the other two do (seeds and berries are also part of the diet), does more of its hunting in the air. It darts out from a perch to catch a flying insect, or flies over the ground and hovers, then pounces. Like other bluebirds, this one nests in cavities, especially old woodpecker diggings; it also uses birdhouses and holes in cliffs and banks.

female

male

finches and the like

Finches and their relatives, such as the small grosbeaks, have strong, stubby seed-cracking beaks and a short, notched tail. They also love to snack on spiders and other arthropods and berries. Like most small passerines, they have a bouncing flight, alternating flapping with gliding on closed wings. Most sing well and are even known to learn songs that are whistled to them. Bright yellow and red are common plumage in this family of birds.

female

male

Feathered fact

Perhaps the best-known winter finch, purple finches bring a dash of bright color and rich, bubbling song to parks and woodlands.

Purple Finch
Carpodacus purpureus

Length: 5 ¼–6 in.

What to look for: male with white belly and raspberry-red head, upperparts, and breast; female brown above, heavily streaked below, with broad white stripe behind eye.

Habitat: mixed woodlands; suburbs and at feeders (migration, winter).

These handsome finches move erratically from place to place, often in large numbers. In winter an area with few or no purple finches one day may have thousands the next. Flocks may consist mostly or solely of brightly colored males or of brown females and immatures. In late summer purple finches begin to molt, and in winter plumage the males' reddish areas appear frosted. With wear, the whitish tinge disappears, revealing the rich breeding color.

male

female

Red Crossbill *Loxia curvirostra*

Length: 5½–6 in.

What to look for: crossed tips of bill; male brick-red, with dark wings and tail; female greenish yellow, lighter below.

Habitat: coniferous forests; occasionally in other woodlands.

The two crossbills—the red- and the white-winged *(Loxia leucoptera)*—are nomads, following the seed crops of conifers or sometimes other forest trees. Their choice of when to nest also seems to depend on the cone supply; they will nest in early spring or even late winter if food is plentiful. A crossbill uses its beak to pry apart the scales of a cone while the tongue extracts the seeds.

House Finch *Carpodacus mexicanus*

Length: 5–5½ in.

What to look for: male with bright red head, breast, and rump; female dull brown, with faintly streaked breast and no eye stripe.

Habitat: deserts, scrubby areas, open forests, farmlands, towns, suburbs; at feeders.

The house finch is an exceptionally adaptable species. Once restricted to the Southwest, it began to extend its range in the 1920s; following the release of caged birds in New York in 1940, house finches spread in the East. The birds nest in all sorts of sites—in holes in trees, among cactus spines, on the beams of buildings, and in the nests of other birds. In the West, Cassin's finch *(Carpodacus cassinii)* may be mistaken for this species or for the purple finch.

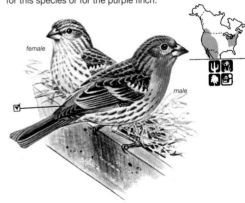
female

male

Feathered fact

American Goldfinches nourish their young with seeds that have been shelled and partially predigested, regurgitating them into the open mouth of their hungry babies.

nonbreeding male

male

female

American Goldfinch
Carduelis tristis

Length: 4–5 in.

What to look for: male bright yellow, with black forehead, wings, and tail; female olive-green above, lighter below; white rump; both sexes yellowish brown in winter; undulating flight.

Habitat: farmlands, weedy fields with scattered trees, river groves, suburbs, parks, at feeders.

Goldfinches breed late in the summer, when thistle-down is available for their tightly woven nests. Feeding flocks can be located by their song, chirps interspersed with *swe-si-iees* or *per-chick-o-rees,* which they also utter in flight. In the West is the lesser goldfinch *(Carduelis psaltria),* with a dark back.

Identifying Birds through Flight

Birds are so unique in their flying patterns that you can actually use this characteristic to identify them. Here are some examples of who flaps, who glides, who hovers, and who exhibits a fanciful bounce.

Goldfinches fly with a bouncy, undulating pattern and often call out in flight, drawing attention to themselves. The reason they bounce is because in between flutters they hold their wings closed for a second, causing them to fall.

Woodpeckers also rise and fall as they fly, flapping their wings furiously and then gliding along. But because they are larger than finches, they don't appear to pop up and down so wildly.

Hummingbirds have one of the most unique styles, hovering in one place for long periods of time with wings flapping at a rate of about 20 beats a second!

Sparrows, wrens, and warblers fly straight ahead without veering off at all.

Crows and ravens look alike from a distance, but don't be fooled—the slow and methodical flapping is the crow; the raven stops flapping frequently to glide.

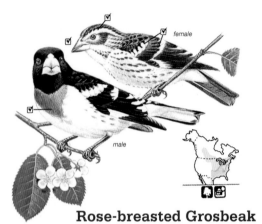

female

male

Rose-breasted Grosbeak
Pheucticus ludovicianus

Length: 7–8 in.

What to look for: heavy bill; male with rose breast patch and black-and-white pattern; female streaked brown, with white eye stripe and wingbars.

Habitat: deciduous woodlands, groves, suburbs.

Conspicuous in his showy plumage, the male rose-breasted grosbeak joins the spring chorus in April or early May. His song has a cheery, lyrical quality, with almost the swing of a march. Though the less colorful female is usually the one to build the loosely constructed nest, some pairs will share the work, and both male and female incubate. If a pair raises a second brood, the male may take charge of the first while his mate sits on the new eggs.

Blue Grosbeak *Guiraca caerulea*

Length: 6–7 in.

What to look for: large conical bill; rusty or buffy wingbars; male blue; female brownish, with dark wings.

Habitat: brushy areas, open woodlands, forests near rivers.

Snakeskins are occasionally woven into the nest of the blue grosbeak, sometimes covering the entire outside; other nesting materials include dry leaves, corn husks, and strips of plastic or newspaper. The female incubates the four eggs for 11 days; the young—fed by both parents, mostly on insects and snails—leave the nest less than two weeks after hatching. For adults fruits, seeds, and other vegetable matter make up perhaps a third of the diet.

male

female

female

male

Evening Grosbeak
Coccothraustes vespertinus

Length: 7–8 in.

What to look for: bill large, light-colored, conical; male yellow-brown, with black tail and black and white wings; female paler, grayish.

Habitat: coniferous forests; other forests and at feeders (migration, winter).

The name evening grosbeak was given this species by an observer who heard a flock at twilight, at a site northwest of Lake Superior. At that time—1823—the evening grosbeak was a western species; since then, it has spread far to the east. One hypothesis is that feeding trays loaded with sunflower seeds may have played a part in this expansion, but reports show that grosbeaks regularly pass up such offerings in favor of boxelder seeds and other wild food.

Black-headed Grosbeak
Pheucticus melanocephalus

Length: 6½–7½ in.

What to look for: heavy whitish bill; male orangish yellow, with black head and black and white wings; female brownish, with facial pattern and streaks.

Habitat: open mixed or deciduous woodlands, forest edges, chaparral, orchards, parks.

This species is the western counterpart of the rose-breasted grosbeak, and their clear, whistled songs are similar. The usual song of the black-headed grosbeak lasts about five seconds but may be longer; a male once performed for seven hours.

female

male

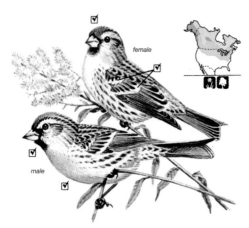

Common Redpoll *Carduelis flammea*

Length: 4 ½–5 ½ in.

What to look for: red forehead; black chin; streaked back and sides; white wingbars; breast and rump pinkish (male).

Habitat: scrub forests, tundra; brushy areas, birch groves, and at feeders (winter).

These northern-breeding "winter finches" occasionally appear at feeders farther south. But often redpolls are much more secretive; they chatter high overhead, become visible for an instant as they dive for a thicket, and then vanish. The pine siskin *(Carduelis pinus),* which flocks with redpolls, has yellow on the wings and tail and no red anywhere.

Pine Grosbeak *Pinicola enucleator*

Length: 7 ½–9 ½ in.

What to look for: large size; conical blackish bill; white wingbars; male mostly rosy red, with blackish wings and tail; female greenish brown above, grayer below.

Habitat: coniferous forests; other woodlands (some winters).

The scientific name of this species translates roughly as "the bird that lives in pines and shells the seeds." But the pine grosbeak has a far more varied diet than the name implies—one that includes beechnuts, crab apples, weed seeds, and insects. Pine grosbeaks breed in the Far North and in mountain areas. In winter they fly to lower latitudes and elevations.

orioles, meadowlarks, and blackbirds

Orioles, meadowlarks, and blackbirds all have various color patterns, from black and iridescent to highly colored plumage. These widespread and familiar birds winter in southern states, but at the first hint of spring, the mature males head north, followed by the females a few weeks later, touching off frenzied courtship displays.

Baltimore/Bullock's Oriole

Icterus galbula/bullockii

Length: 6–7½ in.

What to look for: sharp-pointed bill; male bright orange, with black on head, throat, back, wings, and tail; female and immature pale yellow or orange below, brownish above, with white wingbars.

Habitat: open deciduous woodlands; shade trees in farmlands, towns, cities.

A liquid, whistled song and a flash of brilliant color at the top of a tall tree signal the presence of an oriole. Scientists have recently returned these orioles to two species having merged them in the 1950s. Where the eastern Baltimore and western bullock's ranges overlap in mid-continent, there is some interbreeding, but not enough to consider them valid species. The Baltimore's nest is the familiar deep pouch swinging at the end of a slender limb; its western cousin's is often tied to twigs at the top and sides.

Feathered fact

The Baltimore oriole received its name from the fact that the male's colors resemble those on the coat-of-arms of Lord Baltimore, the British governor of Maryland.

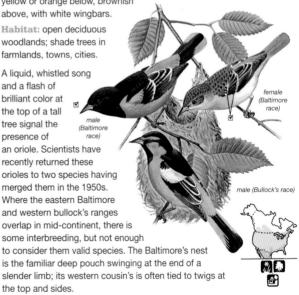

male (Baltimore race)

female (Baltimore race)

male (Bullock's race)

male

female

Scott's Oriole
Icterus parisorum

Length: 6½–8 in.

What to look for: male bright yellow, with black head, upper back, and throat and black on wings and tail; female and immature yellowish green, darker above, with whitish wingbars.

Habitat: deserts; semiarid areas; dry mountain slopes with oaks, pinyons, yucca.

Like other orioles, this western species feeds on insects, fruits, and probably nectar. Like its relatives, it sings throughout the day in the breeding season. And like theirs, is woven of plant fibers. Often hidden among the spiky dead leaves of a yucca, the nest varies in structure according to the surroundings.

Orchard Oriole *Icterus spurius*

Length: 6½–7 in.

What to look for: adult male rusty brown, with black head, throat, upper breast, and upper back and black on wings and tail; first-year male greenish, with black throat; female yellowish green, darker above, with white wingbars.

Habitat: farmlands, orchards, suburbs, towns.

This bird does nest in orchards, where its preference for insects makes it particularly valuable, but it also nests in other habitats. An unusual site was discovered in Louisiana, where nests woven of salt-meadow grasses were suspended from canes in a marsh. The species often seems colonial. On one 7-acre plot in the Mississippi Delta, 114 orchard oriole nests were found in one season. Nearly 20 nests at a time have been noted in a single Louisiana live oak.

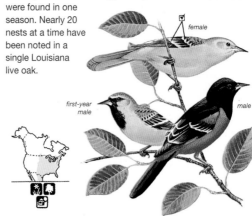

female

first-year male

male

Western Meadowlark

Sturnella neglecta

Length: 8–10½ in.

What to look for: black V across bright yellow underparts; outer tail feathers white; streaked brown above.

Habitat: prairies, meadows, open areas.

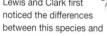
Western Meadowlark

Lewis and Clark first noticed the differences between this species and the eastern meadowlark *(Sturnella magna)*, which look much alike but differ greatly in song. When Audubon rediscovered the western meadowlark in 1843, the scientific name he gave it poked fun at the long time between sightings: it means "neglected meadowlark." Many who have heard the songs of both meadowlarks believe that the sweet, melancholy phrases of the eastern bird cannot compare with the rich, flutelike bubblings of the western.

Eastern Meadowlark

Feathered fact

So alike—in looks, lifestyle, and behavior—are the eastern and western meadowlarks that only an expert would know they aren't the same species. Only their lovely voices, so opposite in tone and song, reveal their true identities.

Bobolink *Dolichonyx oryzivorus*

Length: 5½–7½ in.

What to look for: breeding male black, with back of head yellowish and much white on wings and lower back; other plumages buffy, heavily streaked above.

Habitat: moist open fields, meadows, farmlands, marshes.

The jumbled tinkling of the bobolink's song seems to come from every quarter of the wet meadow or grainfield where the bird nests. The male may be sitting on a weed stalk or fence post or in a tree along the edge; he may be hovering on beating wings or dashing after a female in courtship. Once the breeding season is over, the singing mostly ceases. The male molts into a plumage like that of his mate, and flocks of bobolinks fly to South America, calling pink from time to time as they go.

male

female

Solutions for Nuisance Birds

The term blackbird loosely refers to a group of about 10 different species, including the meadowlarks, bobolinks, grackles, and orioles. The red-winged blackbird is one of the most abundant birds in North America, but it has the reputation of being one of the most troublesome birds as well. Sure, it feeds on harmful insects such as rootworm beetles and corn earworms, but it also causes damage to ripening corn and raids backyard feeders. And starlings, crows, jays, and grackles can be just as much of a nuisance, descending on your yard in large flocks and aggressively driving other bird species out of their nests.

Here are some tips to keep these birds away from your feeders and in your good graces.

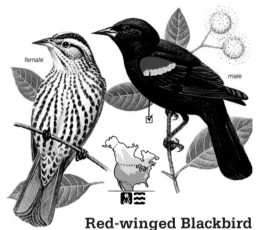

- Never buy seed mixes containing milo. Blackbirds love it, but other birds don't.

- Enclose feeders with chicken wire so only the smaller birds can eat. There are also commercial feeders made specifically to keep blackbirds at bay.

- Thin underbrush and tree branches to discourage flocks of birds from taking up residence and building nests.

- Use feeders that have weighted perches. The feeder will automatically close each time a heavy bird lands on it.

- Stop filling your ground feeders for a week or two. The blackbirds may give up and go elsewhere.

- Cut the perches on your tube feeders so that they are just long enough for your other feathered friends, like finches, chickadees, and titmice.

- Keep birdseed off the ground.

Red-winged Blackbird
Agelaius phoeniceus

Length: 7–9 ½ in.

What to look for: male black, with yellow-bordered red shoulder patch; female dark brown, heavily streaked; immature male like female but with red patch.

Habitat: swamps, marshes, adjacent open areas, farmlands.

The male red-winged blackbird's song is a herald of spring. *Con-ka-ree,* he calls, as if proclaiming victory over winter. Red-wings feed and roost in flocks, but in late summer the flocks vanish. They have retired to some marsh, where the birds hide in the vegetation, molt their flight feathers, and grow new ones. Then the flocks reappear, headed south.

Brown-headed Cowbird
Molothrus ater

Length: 6–8 in.

What to look for: conical bill; male glossy black, with dark brown head; female gray, with paler throat.

Habitat: farmlands, groves, forest edges, river woodlands.

Few birds are as generally disapproved of as the brown-headed cowbird, which lays its eggs in the nests of other birds, particularly flycatchers, sparrows, vireos, and warblers. A newly hatched cowbird quickly grows larger than the rightful nestlings and devours most of the food; it may even push the hosts' eggs or young out of the nest. The foster parents feed the huge intruder until it can fly.

Yellow-headed Blackbird
Xanthocephalus xanthocephalus

Length: 8–10 in.

What to look for: male black, with yellow head and breast and white wing patches; female brown, with dull yellow on face and breast and white throat.

Habitat: freshwater marshes, adjacent open areas.

This handsome species nests over water 2 to 4 feet deep and may abandon a nest if the water level drops. The nests are slung between reed stems and are woven of soggy blades of dead grass. When the grass dries, the nest fabric tightens and the reeds are drawn together, improving the nest's stability. The lining is of leaves, grass, and filmy reed plumes.

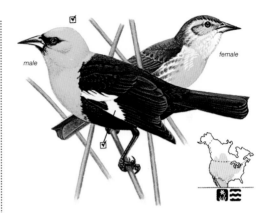

Brewer's Blackbird
Euphagus cyanocephalus

Length: 7½–9½ in.

What to look for: male black, with yellow eye and purple gloss on head; female grayish brown, darker above, with dark eye; tail proportionately shorter than grackle's.

Habitat: open areas, lakeshores.

Two medium-sized blackbirds closely resemble one another—this species and the rusty blackbird *(Euphagus carolinus)*. In winter they may be found in many of the same regions, but the Brewer's blackbird frequents grassy areas, and the rusty the swampy woods. Brewer's gives a strong, rough whistle or a "whirring gurgle"; the rusty calls *tickle-EE*, sounding like a mechanical joint that needs oiling.

Common Grackle
Quiscalus quiscula

Length: 10–12½ in.

What to look for: long keel-shaped tail; long pointed bill; light yellow eye; male glossy black, with purple, bronze, or greenish cast; female less glossy.

Habitat: farmlands, groves, suburbs, parks; usually near water.

Before the trees have begun to leaf out in the North, the common grackles arrive. Soon courting males are posturing in the treetops, puffing their glossy plumage, spreading their long tails, and uttering their rasping *chu-seeck.* Larger species of grackles are the great-tailed *(Quiscalus mexicanus)* of southern farmlands and the boat-tailed *(Quiscalus major)*, a salt-marsh bird.

Feathered fact

Although the song of the common grackle sounds more like a creaking garden gate, these glossy black creatures are still classified as songbirds.

chickadees and titmice

These small, plump birds are a favorite backyard feeder bird because of their friendly, cheery disposition. These exceptionally vocal birds are easy to attract with suet, peanuts, and seed. They are very acrobatic when feeding, flitting about and often taking only one seed at a time from a feeder, flying to another spot to eat it, then returning for more.

Black-capped Chickadee
Parus atricapillus

Length: 4½–5½ in.

What to look for: mostly light gray; black cap and throat; white cheek patch.

Habitat: mixed and deciduous forests, suburbs, parks.

Chickadees that look somewhat alike can often be told apart by their sounds. *Fee-bee,* the black-capped chickadee whistles, the first note of the song a full tone higher than the second. Its call is the familiar *chick-a-dee.* In the Middle West and Southeast the carolina chickadee *(Parus carolinensis)* whistles a longer, more sibilant *su-fee, su-bee,* ending on a low note. Its *chick-a-dee* calls are more rapid.

Boreal Chickadee
Parus hudsonicus

Length: 4½–5 in.

What to look for: brown cap and back; red-brown sides; black throat.

Habitat: northern coniferous forests.

The boreal chickadee seldom wanders far from its northern breeding range. But some winters the "brown caps" move southward in great numbers, probably inspired by a dwindling supply of insect eggs, larvae, and conifer seeds. Boreal chickadees sing their *chick-a-dee* in a drawling, buzzy voice. The chestnut-backed *(Parus rufescens),* found along the Pacific coast and inland to Idaho and Montana, has a shriller, more explosive call.

Mountain Chickadee
Parus gambeli

Length: 4½–5½ in.

What to look for: black line through white cheek patch; black cap and throat.

Habitat: oak-pine and coniferous mountain forests; mixed forests at lower elevations (winter).

All the chickadees nest in cavities, usually in living trees but occasionally in nest boxes and even in holes in the ground. Some species, like the black-capped chickadee, chop out their own holes in rotting wood. The mountain chickadee uses natural cavities or old woodpecker holes that need little enlarging. After the young are raised, this high-altitude species, like the other chickadees, joins mixed flocks of small birds that circulate through the forest as they feed.

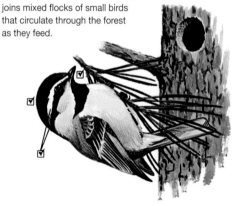

The tufted titmouse has a highly nervous temperament but, on the whole, is a friendly, sociable bird once the young are fledged and gone.

Tufted Titmouse
Parus bicolor

Length: 5½–6 in.

What to look for: gray with buffy flanks; gray crest (black in Texas).

Habitat: deciduous forests, cypress swamps, pine woods, wooded bottomlands, orchards, suburbs.

Long regarded as a southern species, the tufted titmouse has been spreading northward in recent years. Now these tame, confiding birds are familiar visitors at feeders from Michigan to New England. Their ringing song varies; usually it is a rapid two-note whistle—*pe-ter, pe-ter.* Titmice are relatives of the chickadees, and this species has a number of chickadeelike calls. In the West, the plain titmouse *(Parus inornatus),* which lacks the buffy flanks of the tufted, actually does call *tsick-a-dee-dee.*

Winter Birding Basics

Titmice are frequent backyard visitors during the winter. In fact, a surprising number of birds stick around through the coldest months, such as chickadees and nuthatches, woodpeckers, juncos, and the vibrant red cardinal and brilliant blue jay.

Here are some winter birding tips to keep your backyard guests well fed, warm, and happy.

- Add suet nuggets to your seed mix or smear suet or peanut butter onto a tree to give birds an extra boost.

- Chickadees, nuthatches, brown creepers, and woodpeckers all love peanuts. Add some to your seed mix or hang a special peanut feeder to attract extra attention. Peanuts in the shell are favorites of blue jays.

- Fill feeders and birdbaths in the mid-afternoon before the birds go to sleep, so they are well fed to survive the long, cold night. If temps dip below freezing, add some warm water to your birdbath in the morning.

- Brush snow and ice off your feeders and flowers, and keep berry bushes clear.

- Seed blocks and cylinders offer a long, steady source of food even if you don't have time to fill your feeders or if a snowstorm makes it too hard to get outside. Be sure your seed block is heavy on high-fat sunflower and nuts. Avoid seed balls with mostly millet and milo.

- Hang several suet feeders during the winter and make them stable by nestling them against a tree trunk or branch.

Feeding Birds Right from Your Hand

Not only are bushtits one of the smallest passerines in North America, they are also the most gregarious, making them a joy to watch. In fact, with a little prompting—and patience—on your part, you may even get them to eat out of your hand. Some of the more friendly birds include chickadees, common redpolls, downy woodpeckers, evening grosbeaks, goldfinches, jays, nuthatches, and titmice.

Below are some ways bird-watchers have been successful in hand-feeding. But be warned: The birds might start expecting you to feed them by hand every time you go outside!

- At the same time every day, preferably in the early morning, go outside to fill your feeders. Then stand or sit very still nearby— about 10 to 20 feet away—with seed in your hand (or on your hat or shoulder). Do this every day for a few days or weeks, each day getting closer to the feeder.

- Try removing the seed from your feeders and sit still for at least 20 minutes with seed in your hand. Do this every day for a few days.

- To make birds more comfortable around people, put out a wooden dummy early in winter, fully attired, and place some seed on top. (You may be able to purchase a faux birder in a local garden center, or search online.) The birds will get so accustomed to eating from it they will begin to think all people are a source of food.

Bushtit
Psaltriparus minimus

Length: 3–4 in.

What to look for: small grayish bird with long tail; brown cap (Rocky Mountain race with gray cap and brown cheeks); male in extreme Southwest with black mask.

Habitat: mixed woodlands; stands of scrub oak, pinyon, or juniper; chaparral.

Bushtits are small, inconspicuous birds that build elaborate nests. A pair begins by constructing a more or less horizontal rim between adjacent twigs. With this as a frame, the birds weave a small sack and gradually stretch and strengthen it, working mostly from inside. A hood and an entrance hole are added at the top. Materials vary with the locality, but usually the nest is held together with spiderweb and decorated with bits of moss and lichen.

Feathered fact
Bushtits are the masters of tumbling and trapeze artistry, and any bush or tree will do for a stage.

Wrentit *Chamaea fasciata*

Length: 5–6 in.

What to look for: brown bird with streaked breast; tail long, rounded, often erect; light eye.

Habitat: chaparral, brushy areas, suburbs, parks.

Once it is located by its loud, whistling song, this little bird is difficult to watch. It seldom flies any distance or perches in the open, but instead moves about stealthily in dense brush. Much of what is known about the wrentit is due to an observer who studied a population in a California canyon. Among other discoveries, she found that at night roosting pairs sit side by side and shuffle their body feathers so that they become enveloped in a single bundle of plumage.

Verdin *Auriparus flaviceps*

Length: 4–4½ in.

What to look for: small size; grayish, with yellow on head (paler on female) and chestnut shoulder patch.

Habitat: semiarid or arid regions with scattered thorny scrub and mesquite.

A remarkable nest builder, the verdin weaves a round, long-lasting shell of stout, thorny twigs. The nest is lined with plant down and other plant material, spider silk, and feathers. Inside the entrance is a high "doorstep" that discourages intruders. The verdin usually locates its nest conspicuously in a cactus, thorny bush, or small tree, choosing a fork at the end of a low branch. These structures are also used for roosting and winter shelter.

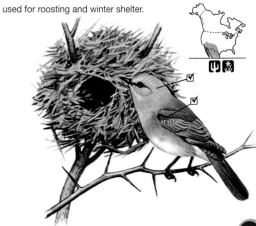

sparrows, juncos, towhees, and longspurs

These small songbirds typically have short, thick, triangular bills and chunky bodies. Found throughout all of North America, these birds are generally so shy and secretive that they are hard to tell apart. Much of their time is spent foraging around under thick underbrush looking for food or making short, quick flights between patches for cover to hide from predators, but once in a while they climb onto branches to deliver a quick song, especially in the spring.

immature

Feathered fact
Pesky and tireless, chipping sparrows nip at horses' tails for hairs to be woven into nests.

Chipping Sparrow
Spizella passerina

Length: 4½–5½ in.

What to look for: reddish cap; white stripe above eye; black eye streak; pale grayish below; immature with streaky brown cap.

Habitat: open woodlands, forest edges, farmlands, orchards, suburbs, parks.

The "chippy" is named for its song—a trill or string of musical chips, varying from quite long to very brief. It normally sings from a perch in a tree, often an evergreen. Evergreens are also favorite nesting sites, although the birds may be found raising young in orchard trees, in dooryard vines and shrubbery, and occasionally even on the ground.

American Tree Sparrow
Spizella arborea

Length: 5½–6½ in.

What to look for: reddish cap and eye streak; dark spot in center of pale gray breast.

Habitat: subarctic areas with stunted trees; brushy areas, grasslands, woodland edges, weedy fields, and at feeders (winter).

Preferring underbrush and shrubs to trees, American tree sparrows nest on the ground in dense thickets in the far North. Whether they appear in large numbers in more southerly regions during winter months depends on the severity of the weather. When the warmth of spring returns, the birds' tinkling song can be heard before they depart for their northern nesting grounds.

Field Sparrow
Spizella pusilla

Length: 5–6 in.

What to look for: pinkish bill; reddish cap; buffy below; immature with streaked cap and buffy chest band.

Habitat: brushy and weedy grasslands, meadows, forest edges.

immature

The sweet song of the field sparrow is a series of whistled notes delivered slowly at first and then accelerated into a rapid run. In spring, males establish territories by singing and by chasing their neighbors; once a male is mated, he sings far less than before. Early in the season, nest sites are on the ground or only a short distance above it. As the season advances and the pairs begin second and third families, fewer ground nests are attempted. Nests, however, are seldom more than 3 feet above the ground.

Brewer's Sparrow
Spizella breweri

Length: 4½–5 in.

What to look for: finely streaked buffy cap; gray cheek patch; very pale below.

Habitat: sagebrush, other brushy areas, alpine meadows; weedy fields (winter).

A shy bird, the Brewer's sparrow tends to keep out of sight, and its nest is even harder to find. One observer wrote of scaring up an incubating bird; although it flushed about 3 feet in front of his foot and he saw it leave, he had to get down on hands and knees and inspect the ground inch by inch in order to discover the nest. The Brewer's sparrow migrates in flocks with the clay-colored sparrow *(Spizella pallida),* a confusingly similar species with a more eastern range.

House Sparrow (English Sparrow)
Passer domesticus

Length: 5–6 in.

What to look for: male with black, whitish, gray, and reddish on head and breast; female brownish above, grayer below.

Habitat: farms, suburbs, cities.

Most people regret the efforts made in the 19th century to transplant the house sparrow from Europe. House sparrows, which belong to a completely different family from our native sparrows, drive bluebirds, wrens, and other songbirds from nesting sites; they tear up nests, destroy eggs, and toss out nestlings. The species reached its peak early in this century. Since then, numbers have declined, probably because of the scarcity of horses and therefore of the waste horse feed eaten by the birds.

male

female

immature

Song Sparrow
Melospiza melodia

Length: 5–7 in.

What to look for: heavily streaked below, with dark central breast spot; longish tail; immature more finely streaked.

Habitat: forest edges, brushy areas, thickets, hedgerows, parks, beaches.

Ornithologists recognize more than 30 subspecies of the remarkably adaptable song sparrow. The birds vary considerably in size, with the largest races 40 percent bigger than the smallest. The color ranges from reddish or dark brown to pale gray. The song typically begins with several regularly spaced notes, followed by a trill, then a jumble of notes. Because song sparrows seem to learn the structure of their music from other song sparrows, local "dialects" are common. And each song sparrow has a variety of private versions; no two individuals sing the same tune.

Swamp Sparrow *Melospiza georgiana*

Length: 4½–5½ in.

What to look for: reddish cap; gray face and breast; whitish throat; buffy or pale tawny flanks; rusty wings.

Habitat: brushy swamps, bogs, marshes; fields, weedy edges (migration, winter).

Within its breeding range this is one of the last diurnal birds to fall silent at night and among the first to tune up in the morning, long before daybreak. Sometimes swamp sparrows keep singing through the night. Their musical trilling—richer than the chipping sparrow's but otherwise quite similar—sounds from all over the northern marshes where they nest. One authority writes that some swamp sparrow phrases are double. The birds sing two different songs on different pitches at once—"the higher notes being slow and sweet, and the lower notes faster and somewhat guttural."

Golden-crowned Sparrow
Zonotrichia atricapilla

Length: 6–7 in.

What to look for: large size; crown yellow, with black border (immature with duller, brown-bordered crown); breast gray.

Habitat: Arctic and mountain areas with stunted trees; spruce woodlands, brushy slopes; thickets, scrub areas (winter).

This western sparrow is most often seen during migration or in winter, when it may be common on patios and in gardens. It feeds on seeds, seedlings, buds, and blossoms. This bird is large; the fox sparrow and Harris's sparrow (*Zonotrichia querula),* a black-throated species with a mid-continental range, are the only bigger North American sparrows.

White-crowned Sparrow
Zonotrichia leucophrys

Length: 5½–7 in.

What to look for: crown broadly striped with black and white (light and dark brown on immature); gray breast; pink or yellowish bill; pale throat.

Habitat: mountain thickets, areas with scattered brush and trees; roadsides, suburbs (winter).

The trim, elegant white-crowned sparrow breeds in brushy, open terrain, whether in the subarctic, in western mountains, or along the Pacific Coast. The nest site is usually on or near the ground. Male and female approach the nest differently: The male flies in directly; the female lands 10 to 15 feet away, then moves in by stages, pausing often to perch.

immature

Feathered fact

In its northern habitat this sparrow is often seen scratching for seeds in the snow.

Savannah Sparrow
Passerculus sandwichensis

Length: 4–6 in.

What to look for: streaked above, heavily streaked below; light stripe above eye; short tail; varies from pale to dark.

Habitat: tundra, prairies, meadows, salt marshes, beaches.

When alarmed, the Savannah sparrow seems to prefer running through the grass to flying. When it does fly up, it usually skims over the grass very briefly, then drops out of sight. Males often sing from a weed-top perch. The song— *tsip-tsip-tsip-seeeee-saaaaay*—ends in a two-part trill that at a distance is all that can be heard. Savannah is a fair description of the bird's habitat, but the name actually refers to the Georgia city where the first specimen was found.

immature

White-throated Sparrow
Zonotrichia albicollis

Length: 5½–6½ in.

What to look for: white throat; gray breast; black and white striped crown, often with yellow patch in front of eye (crown of immature with brown and buff stripes).

Habitat: woodlands with dense brush; brushy areas, forest edges (migration, winter).

The white-throat is often nicknamed the Canada Bird or the Peabody Bird, in imitation of a typical song, written as *"Oh, sweet Canada, Canada, Canada,"* or *"Poor Sam Peabody, Peabody, Peabody."* But there are regional dialects among white-throated sparrows, as well as marked individual variations. Because the white-throat whistles its sweet song loudly and slowly, these variations are especially noticeable.

Grasshopper Sparrow
Ammodramus savannarum

Length: 4–5 in.

What to look for: short-necked appearance; flat head; short tail; buffy, rather unstreaked breast; streaked back.

Habitat: grasslands, meadows, weedy fields, marshes.

The usual song of the grasshopper sparrow consists of a few faint ticks followed by a long, dry trill. The bird sounds like a grasshopper. It also eats grasshoppers, and so the name is doubly appropriate. Grasshopper sparrows nest in colonies in open grasslands, laying eggs in a slight hollow at the base of a short tuft of vegetation. The nest is difficult to find because the female leaves and approaches it on foot, under cover.

Fox Sparrow *Passerella iliaca*

Length: 6–7¼ in.

What to look for: large size; rusty tail; brown, red-brown, or gray above; streaked below, with large central spot.

Habitat: scrubby trees of subarctic and mountain slopes; forest undergrowth; thickets, farmlands, parks (migration, winter).

The husky fox sparrow scratches vigorously for seeds, small fruits, and insects among fallen leaves, jumping forward and back with both feet and spraying litter in all directions. Its summer food is mostly insects and other animals; Audubon reported seeing fox sparrows eat tiny shellfish in coastal Newfoundland and Labrador. Its voice is as distinctive as its appearance. The song is a series of rich, often slurred whistles run together in a short "sentence." Indeed, the general impression is that of a conversation.

gray form

red-brown form

Vesper Sparrow
Pooecetes gramineus

Length: 5–6 in.

What to look for: white outer tail feathers; white eye ring; reddish shoulder patch; brown above, with darker streaks; white below, with brown streaks.

Habitat: open fields, grasslands with scattered trees, sagebrush areas.

This is a ground-nesting species: it makes a small depression in the earth and fills it with grasses, roots, and sometimes hair. The female lays from three to five eggs, which—if they escape predation—hatch within two weeks. The young are ready to leave the nest less than two weeks later. The vesper sparrow often sings its sweet song at dusk—hence, its name.

Birds and Their Courtship Techniques

Vesper sparrows are monogamous and will often raise two broods in a season. In fact, these adult pairs stay together year-round and usually for life, unless one dies, and only then will the vesper sparrow look for another mate.

Until DNA testing techniques came about in the '80s, most people assumed this was common practice for birds, but scientists now claim that most species are far from monogamous and actually behave very much like people: Birds meet and carry on a courtship that includes dinner dates, dancing, and just hanging out together. The males, especially, sing, show off a lot, and wear flashy adornments just to impress females. If the birds like each other, they become a pair, build a nest, raise youngsters, school them, and send them off to form their own families.

As for our common backyard birds, like goldfinches, chickadees, and robins, marriage bonds are less committed. They often last for only one breeding season or for one nesting period. Some of our most common birds, such as red-winged blackbirds, house wrens, and ruby-throated hummingbirds, have communal relationships in which one male and several females all nest at the same time.

Northern cardinals, though, appear to have a longer-lasting marriage than most songbirds. During winter the two are not so kind to each other, but come spring the male's fancy takes a new direction. Instead of chasing the female away from the bird feeder, as he does all winter, he offers her a sunflower seed and the courtship starts again.

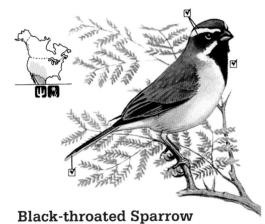

Black-throated Sparrow
Amphispiza bilineata

Length: 4½–5½ in.

What to look for: black throat; white lines above and below eye patch; plain gray back; white outer tail feathers.

Habitat: brushy deserts, semiarid areas.

This species sometimes competes for habitat with the sage sparrow *(Amphispiza belli),* but the black-throated sparrow is more of a true desert bird and is regularly found far from any water hole or stream. Both have nestlings with pale downy plumage, as do other species that nest in hot, open areas. This coloration is believed to help the young survive, by reflecting rather than absorbing light.

Lark Sparrow *Chondestes grammacus*

Length: 5½–6½ in.

What to look for: facial pattern; clear breast with black spot (immature with streaked breast); tail with white border.

Habitat: prairies, open woodlands, fields, farmlands.

Lark sparrows collect in flocks to feed, but the males are extremely pugnacious near their nests. They fight each other on the ground or in the air, and often these battles turn into free-for-alls. One observer reported seeing five or six males fighting together in midair, "so oblivious to their surroundings that [they] nearly hit me in the face."

"Oregon junco"
(a western race)

"slate-colored junco"
(eastern race)

Dark-eyed Junco *Junco hyemalis*

Length: 5–6½ in.

What to look for: white outer tail feathers; light pink bill; white belly; rest of plumage slate-gray (with or without white wingbars) or rusty brown with dark head and pinkish-brown flanks.

Habitat: coniferous and mixed forests; forest edges and at feeders (winter).

Until recently, the birds shown above were considered separate species. A third form was the white-winged junco, found in a limited range in the West. All three are now believed to be races of a single species and have been "lumped" under the name dark-eyed junco. A fourth form, the gray-headed, common in the Southwest, was recently added to this species.

Eastern/Spotted Towhee
Pipilo erythrophthalmus/maculatus

Length: 7–8 in.

What to look for: male mostly black and white, with rufous flanks and white on wings and tail; white spots on back (West); female with brown instead of black.

Habitat: thickets, open forests, brushy fields, chaparral, suburbs, parks.

A loud, buzzy *shree* or *shrank* from the underbrush and vigorous scratching in the leaves announce the presence of an eastern towhee. Its song is often transcribed as *drink-your-teeeee.* In the West, the spotted towhee behaves much the same, and it sounds much like its eastern cousin. There are other towhee species in the West; the California (*Pipilo crissalis*) and the canyon (*Pipilo fuscus*) were once considered one species. They are common in suburban yards.

female (East)

male (East)

male (West)

nonbreeding male

nonbreeding female

breeding male

Lapland Longspur *Calcarius lapponicus*

Length: 5½–6½ in.

What to look for: some plumages with chestnut nape; white outer tail feathers; breeding male with black head, throat, and breast; nonbreeding male with white throat and black breast band; female finely streaked.

Habitat: tundra; prairies, meadows, beaches (winter).

The dramatic summer dress of this species is never seen by most people, for the Lapland longspur nests in the far North. There, ornithologists have noticed that its breeding activities are remarkably synchronized. Most males start singing at once, most pairs mate at the same time, and most egg laying begins on the same date. Most adults and young also follow a common schedule when they molt before migration.

Chestnut-collared Longspur
Calcarius ornatus

Length: 5½–6½ in.

What to look for: tail white with black central triangle; breeding male with bold facial pattern, chestnut nape, and black underparts; female and nonbreeding male streaked buffy brown.

Habitat: prairies, plains, large fields.

Loose colonies of chestnut-collared longspurs breed in short-grass prairies or weedy fields. The conspicuous male defends his territory by perching on a stone or weed stalk and by singing in flight. The protectively colored female digs a slight hollow near a grass tuft and lines it, mainly with grass. She alone incubates, but both parents supply the young with food. Though the summer diet includes insects, seeds are the mainstay the rest of the year.

male

female

jays and crows

Known as nuisance birds because they travel in flocks and frequently raid backyard feeders, jays and crows are actually among the most intelligent birds on Earth. They warn when hunters are hiding in ambush, pass the word on new sources of food, and are wonderfully resilient to man-changed environments, moving easily from forests to farmlands and suburbs to city parks.

Feathered fact

The blue jay's tameness, plus its constant curiosity, make it an ideal bird for observation and for stimulating exercises in separating fact from stereotype.

Blue Jay *Cyanocitta cristata*

Length: 9½–12 in.

What to look for: pointed crest; black "necklace"; bright blue above, with white on wings and tail.

Habitat: woodlands, farmlands, suburbs, city parks.

This handsome, noisy bird is known for its raucous voice and the wide variety of its calls, cries, and screams. But like other jays, it also has a "whisper song," a series of faint whistles and soft, sweet notes delivered from a perch hidden in foliage. Blue jays are omnivorous, feeding on (among other things) fruits, seeds, nuts, insects, birds' eggs, small birds, mice, treefrogs, snails, and even fish. In spring and fall these jays migrate in flocks that sometimes number in the hundreds.

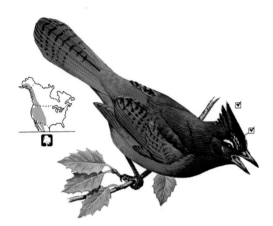

Steller's Jay *Cyanocitta stelleri*

Length: 11½–13½ in.

What to look for: crest long, sharp-pointed, blackish; face streaked with white; upper back and breast blackish; dark blue wings and tail.

Habitat: pine-oak and coniferous forests.

A characteristic habit of jays is the way they land on a tree near the bottom and then work upward, hopping from branch to branch until they reach the top. Then they leave, perhaps to repeat the maneuver. Steller's jays, like their relatives, build bulky nests of dead leaves and twigs, usually near the trunk of a conifer.

Scrub Jay *Aphelocoma coerulescens*

Length: 9½–12 in.

What to look for: no crest; head, wings, and tail blue; mostly white below.

Habitat: scrub oak chaparral; pinyon-juniper woodlands; palmetto-pine thickets (Florida).

The scrub jays have separated into several forms in Florida and the West. The wide gap in distribution may have been caused by changes in climate, habitat, or food supply. The scrub jays have become different enough to be considered three species: the Florida scrub jay *(Aphelocoma coerulescens),* the western scrub jay *(Aphelocoma californica),* and the island scrub jay *(Aphelocoma insularis).*

Clark's Nutcracker
Nucifraga columbiana

Length: 12–13 in.

What to look for: body light gray; wings and tail black, with white patches; bill long, pointed.

Habitat: coniferous forests near tree line; lower slopes, isolated groves.

William Clark, of the Lewis and Clark expedition, thought this bird was a woodpecker, but the leading American ornithologist of the day, Alexander Wilson, called it a crow. Clark's nutcracker has the woodpecker's bounding flight at times; at other times it flies more directly, like a crow. It pecks at cones and nuts like a woodpecker and robs the nests of other birds, as crows do.

Gray Jay
Perisoreus canadensis

Length: 9½–12½ in.

What to look for: gray with dark nape, white throat, and white forehead; immature gray, with light "mustache."

Habitat: coniferous forests, upland aspen and birch groves.

This is the Wis-ka-tjon of the Indians, the Whiskey Jack or Camp Robber of the white trappers, and the Canada Jay of old-time ornithology. A boldly confident bird, it hangs around forest camps, exploring even inside the tents and stealing food, soap, candles, and tobacco. Gray jays nest while snow still covers the ground, and often line the nest with feathers for warmth. They seldom migrate except in "famine" years, when flocks of them drift south.

adult

immature

Feathered fact

The gray jay is known as a scavenger. It may boldly alight on a plate or a frying pan to filch a tasty meal. Indians were known to say that the gray jay eats anything—including fur caps and moccasins.

Common Crow

Common Raven

Yellow-billed Magpie

American Crow *Corvus brachyrhynchos*

Length: 16–20 in.

What to look for: glossy black, with black bill, legs, and feet; rounded wings and tail.

Habitat: forests; woods near water; open areas; farmlands; suburbs.

Judged by human standards, crows are perhaps the most intelligent of birds. They can count at least to three or four; they quickly learn new information; they appear to have a complex language and well-developed social structure. North America has three kinds, the American crow and two smaller species usually found near the shore— the northwestern and the fish crow *(Corvus caurinus and ossifragus).* A Mexican species also visits Texas. The common and the Chihuahuan raven *(Corvus corax and cryptoleucus),* larger birds with wedge-shaped tails, are sometimes mistaken for crows.

Black-billed Magpie
Pica pica

Length: 17½–21½ in.

What to look for: tail long, tapering, metallic greeen; bold black and white pattern in flight.

Habitat: open forests, brushy areas of prairies and foothills; bottomland groves; ranches.

This conspicuous, long-tailed species constructs a particularly strong nest in a bush or low in a tree. Sticks, often thorny, make up the base and walls. Mud or fresh dung mixed with vegetation is packed inside, and the cup is lined with roots, stems, and hair. Over the nest the birds build a dome of sticks—again, often thorny. The yellow-billed magpie *(Pica nuttalli)* of California builds the same sort of nest.

waxwings and starlings

The flight of waxwings and starlings is strong and direct, and the flocks resemble each other overhead. Both eat fruit and berries year-round and display confident, bold dispositions, the waxwing swooping in to visit backyard gardens and trees to look for berries or to drink from fountains and birdbaths. However, the starling takes its gregariousness a step further, consuming the fruit of farmers and robbing purple martins and bluebirds of their nesting holes.

immature

Cedar Waxwing *Bombycilla cedrorum*

Length: 5½–7½ in.

What to look for: crest; mostly soft brown, with black face pattern, yellow-tipped tail, and red spots on wing; immature with brown streaks.

Habitat: open forests, areas with scattered trees, wooded swamps, orchards, suburbs.

Cedar waxwings are a particularly sociable species. It is not unusual to see a row of them perched on a branch, passing a berry or an insect down the line and back again, bill to bill, in a ceremony that ends when one swallows the food. The birds wander in flocks whose arrivals and departures are unpredictable. Flocks of the northwestern Bohemian waxwing *(Bombycilla garrulus)* are also erratic, and may suddenly appear well outside their normal range.

male

Phainopepla *Phainopepla nitens*

Length: 6½–7½ in.

What to look for: crest; male glossy black, with white wing patches conspicuous in flight; female and immature dingy gray, with pale wing patches.

Habitat: scrubby arid and semiarid areas with scattered trees; oak groves in canyons.

The name phainopepla means "shining robe," a reference to the bright, silky plumage of the male. The species is believed to be related to the waxwings, and like them it is both a fly catcher and a fruit eater. The phainopepla's shallow nest, made of small twigs, sticky leaves and blossoms, and spiderweb, is usually placed in a fork of a mesquite or other small tree. The male generally begins the project, and his mate does the rest of the job.

European Starling
Slurnus vulgaris

Length: 7–8½ in.

What to look for: long pointed bill; short, square tail; black overall, with greenish and purple gloss (nonbreeding with light spots); immature brownish, darker above.

Habitat: farmlands, open woodlands, brushy areas, towns, cities.

In 1890 the efforts to introduce this European bird to North America succeeded, and descendants of the 100 birds released in New York City began to spread across the land. The starling's habit of gathering in huge roosts has made it a pest in many areas, and it deprives many hole-nesting species of their homes. It does, however, eat many destructive insects.

nonbreeding

breeding

shrikes and vireos

A distinctive feature of the shrike is its hook-tipped bill. Similar in appearance to the northern mockingbird, its song consists of disjointed, harsh notes. Shrikes feast on insects, lizards, small rodents, and small birds and often impale prey on thorns or barbed wire. Vireos look very similar to the shrike with its hooked bill and long tail, but most can easily be distinguished by the presence of white wingbars.

Loggerhead Shrike
Lanius ludovicianus

Length: 7–9½ in.

What to look for: gray above, with black mask; paler below; bill short, heavy; wings black, with white patches; outer tail feathers white.

Feathered fact

The distinctive tooth on its bill underscores the shrike's fearsome reputation as a hunter.

Habitat: open areas with scattered trees and shrubs.

Both the loggerhead shrike and the rarer northern shrike *(Lanius excubitor)* are nicknamed "butcher-birds." They kill insects, snakes, rodents, and small birds, then impale them on thorns or barbed wire or jam them into twig forks. Often they build up sizable larders. Evidently, however, the purpose of this habit is more than storage against lean times. For although the shrikes have hooked, hawklike bills, they lack powerful, hawklike feet and apparently must fix the prey on something firm before tearing it with their bill.

Warbling Vireo *Vireo gilvus*

Length: 4½–5½ in.

What to look for: no conspicuous markings; grayish green above, white below.

Habitat: open mixed and deciduous forests; groves; orchards; shade trees in towns and suburbs.

Twelve species of vireos nest in North America. The warbling vireo and a few others have continent-wide ranges. Others— the eastern white-eyed *(Vireo griseus)* and western Bell's *(Vireo bellii),* for example—are limited to smaller areas. All are noted for the leisurely pace of their activity, compared with that of kinglets and warblers, with which they are often seen on migration. They also have thicker bills.

Solitary Vireo *Vireo solitarius*

Length: 4½–6 in.

What to look for: white "spectacles"; white wingbars; gray or bluish head; greenish or gray above, mostly white below.

Habitat: mixed or coniferous forests.

Like all the vireos, the solitary hangs its nest by the rim in a twiggy fork. As a structure, too, the nest is typical of vireos', consisting of bits of bark and moss, leaves, and fine materials such as wool and feathers. The parents sing to each other as they share incubation and early care of the young. The song is bright and measured, not unlike a pure robin song.

Feathered fact

The red-eyed vireo is the all-time
endurance vocalist champion:
On a single day one was recorded
singing more than 22,000
individual songs.

Red-eyed Vireo
Vireo olivaceus

Length: 5–6½ in.

What to look for: white eye stripe; gray cap;
greenish above, white below; no wingbars.

Habitat: deciduous woodlands, open areas with
scattered trees, suburbs.

During the breeding season the male red-eyed vireo is a persistent singer, delivering lengthy passages of short two- to six-note
phrases. The bird tends to go on so long that he used to be
nicknamed "Preacher." Usually he sings at normal volume, but in
courtship he also has a "whisper song," sometimes quite different
in character from the regular song.

Did You Know...

...that a group of red-eyed vireos is collectively
known as a hangover? Or that a group of crows
can be referred to as a hover, muster, parcel or
parliament? Some terms are well
known—such as flock or flight—
but here are some others that
may not be as familiar:

- A *chain* of bobolinks
- A *gulp* of cormorants
- A *dole* of doves
- A *charm* of finches
- A *bevy* of larks
- A *tittering* or *tiding* of magpies
- A *stare* or *wisdom* of owls
- A *covey* of ptarmigan
- A *host* or *knot* of sparrows
- A *chattering* or *murmation* of starlings
- A *descent* of woodpeckers
- A *herd* of wrens
- A *marathon* of roadrunners
- A *brood* or *clutch* of chicks
- A *party, scold,* or *band* of jays

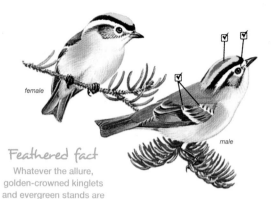

female

male

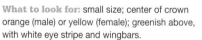

kinglets, wrens, and gnatcatchers

These small, energetic birds feast on insects and are seen throughout North America. Although mainly inconspicuous because of their dull plumage, the wrens and gnatcatchers are known for their cocked tails, the latter having a much longer, black-and-white tail that sticks straight up. Kinglets resemble titmice and are often seen socializing with warblers and chickadees. All have the typical insectivore's long, sharp bill.

Feathered fact

Whatever the allure, golden-crowned kinglets and evergreen stands are inextricably linked.

Golden-crowned Kinglet
Regulus satrapa

Length: 3–4 in.

What to look for: small size; center of crown orange (male) or yellow (female); greenish above, with white eye stripe and wingbars.

Habitat: coniferous forests; other forests, thickets (migration, winter).

Restless, flitting movements and a very small size are good signs that the bird you are looking at is a kinglet. Scarcely pausing to perch, kinglets glean small insects and their eggs from leaves and bark. In its fluttering flight the golden-crowned kinglet utters a high, thin *sssst,* which is often repeated several times as a phrase.

Ruby-crowned Kinglet
Regulus calendula

Length: 3½–4 in.

What to look for: small size; greenish above, with white eye ring and wingbars; red crown (male); often flicks wings.

Habitat: coniferous forests; other woodlands, thickets (migration, winter).

The ruby crown of this kinglet is worn only by the males, and even on them it is not always evident. (The amount of red that shows seems to depend on how agitated the kinglet is.) Though a mere mite of a bird, it has a loud and varied song, and ornithologists from Audubon on have mentioned how astonished they were the first time they heard a ruby-crowned kinglet sing.

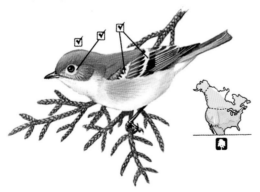

Carolina Wren
Thryothorus ludovicianus

Length: 4½–5½ in.

What to look for: wide white eye stripe; rufous above, with white throat and tawny sides.

Habitat: forests with dense undergrowth; scrubby areas; thickets; brush near water.

The loud, ringing call of the Carolina wren is one of the most common sounds of southeastern woods, where it is heard even in winter. The call is usually a series of double or triple notes, written as *cheery, cheery, cheery* or *tea-kettle, tea-kettle, tea-kettle.* The bird has been called "mocking wren" because it sometimes sounds like a catbird, a kingfisher, or certain other kinds of birds.

House Wren *Troglodytes aedon*

Length: 4–5 in.

What to look for: gray-brown above, lighter below, with barring on wings and tail; tail often held erect.

Habitat: open woodlands, forest edges, shrubby areas, suburbs, parks.

House wrens are aggressive and adaptable nesters. They will build their nests in just about any container left out in the open—flowerpot, empty tin can, pocket of an old coat—as well as tree holes and nest boxes. They often bully other birds, ejecting them from nest sites and even destroying eggs and young. Two broods a season are raised. The male frequently changes partners in mid-season, so that while his original mate is still feeding chicks, another female is sitting on new eggs.

Winter Wren
Troglodytes troglodytes

Length: 3–4 in.

What to look for: small size; reddish brown, with dark barring on flanks; very short tail.

Habitat: coniferous and mixed forests with heavy undergrowth, often near streams; wooded swamps.

The song of the winter wren is clear, rapid, and very high in pitch, often with notes beyond the range of human ears. The wren sings along at 16 notes a second, stringing beautiful, tinkling passages into long pieces. It sings over the sound of surf on remote Alaskan islands, where it nests on cliffs and rocky slopes near the shore. Elsewhere it is most often a bird of the deep woods, nesting in the earth that clings to the roots of fallen trees, under standing roots, or in crevices between rocks.

Bewick's Wren *Thryomanes bewickii*

Length: 4½–5½ in.

What to look for: white eye stripe; brown above, white below; tail long, with white spots on outer feathers.

Habitat: woodlands, brushy areas, chaparral, suburbs.

Audubon named this species for a British friend, Thomas Bewick (pronounced "buick"), whose wood engravings of birds were famous in his day. Though somewhat larger than the house wren, Bewick's wren is less aggressive, and it usually loses out when the two species compete for space. Its diet, like that of all wrens, consists almost entirely of insects, spiders, and other small invertebrates; Bewick's wren in particular is credited with destroying many injurious species such as scale insects and bark beetles.

Rock Wren
Salpinctes obsoletus

Length: 4½–6 in.

What to look for: upper parts grayish brown, with rufous rump; throat and breast white, finely streaked with brown.

Habitat: deserts; high, dry meadows; rocky areas.

The rock wren is a loud, rough-voiced, and garrulous singer with the habit of repeating itself. One listener wrote: *"Keree, keree, keree, keree, he says. Chair, chair, chair, chair, deedle, deedle, deedle, deedle, tur, tur, tur, tur, keree, keree, keree, trrrrrrrrr."* The rock wren nests in holes in the earth, between boulders, or under loose stones, often on slopes. It usually paves the floor beneath and around its nest with small stones and sometimes also with bones and assorted trash. Another western species of about the same size is the white-breasted canyon wren (*Catherpes mexicanus*).

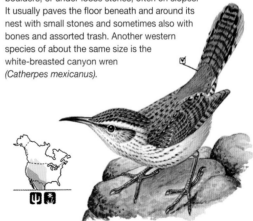

Are You a Birder or Bird-Watcher?

You may get excited at seeing a cactus wren foraging along in your backyard leaves looking for insects, or you may become more involved in its behavior, observing that when the female cactus wren is incubating on a clutch of eggs, the male wren spends his time building another nest to be used for a second clutch of eggs. You may even take note that the cactus wren's nest is the size and shape of a football with an opening at one end.

Watching birds is a hobby that can involve your interest at many levels. For some it's a casual look at the wild world around us. For others it's an enjoyable opportunity to learn interesting facts, like nesting and rearing, to help understand birds better. The terms bird-watcher and birder are used to distinguish the level of interest one has and the knowledge and skills that have been gained. In general, birders are the more involved and more deeply informed of the two.

A simple interest in birds requires little by way of formal education, equipment, or technique. A pair of binoculars is all that you'll need. But as your interest in bird-watching grows, you may want to get involved with other birding groups and attend events. Birders are always happy to share their knowledge. Start a life list to help you keep track of the birds you have seen over time. Or search online for a list and print it out. Then you can check the species off as you see them.

Cactus Wren
Campylorhynchus brunneicapillus

Length: 6–8½ in.

What to look for: large size; white eye stripe; throat and breast heavily spotted with black; wings and tail barred with black.

Habitat: brushy desert areas with cactus, yucca, and mesquite.

The largest wren is a bird of arid, low-altitude country where cacti are plentiful. Its nest is conspicuous—a domed affair with a tunnel entrance 5 or 6 inches long. The whole structure, woven of plant fibers, leaves, and twigs, is shaped rather like a flask lying on its side. Typically, it is placed in the arms of a big cactus or on a branch of a thorny bush or mesquite tree. A pair of cactus wrens will maintain several nests at one time and may raise three broods a year, changing nests at the beginning of each cycle. After the young have left, the adults continue to make repairs, since the nests are used as winter roosts.

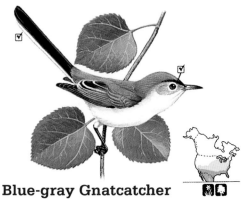

Blue-gray Gnatcatcher
Polioptila caerulea

Length: 4–5 in.

What to look for: slim, long-tailed bird; blue-gray above, white below; tail blackish, with white outer feathers; white eye ring.

Habitat: mixed and oak forests, chaparral, open pinyon-juniper forests, thickets and groves along rivers.

This tiny bird darts from perch to perch, uttering its thin, mewing spee, flicking its long tail, and feeding on tiny insects. In the breeding season the male has a soft, warbling song. He assists with the building of the nest, which may be located as low as 3 feet or as high as 80 feet above the ground. The structure is roughly the shape of an acorn with the top hollowed out, and it consists of various fine materials, including plant down, petals, feathers, and hair.

American Dipper
Cinclus mexicanus

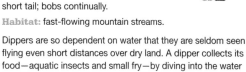

Length: 5½–8 in.

What to look for: stocky bird; slate-gray, with white eye ring; legs long, yellowish; short tail; bobs continually.

Habitat: fast-flowing mountain streams.

Dippers are so dependent on water that they are seldom seen flying even short distances over dry land. A dipper collects its food—aquatic insects and small fry—by diving into the water and wading submerged along the bottom. In Alaska dippers have been seen flitting around the icy edges of open water holes and diving when the air temperature was far below zero. The nest is built under a streambank or waterfall.

kingfishers and swifts

The solitary, large-headed kingfisher keeps to the air, hovering over water and plunging headfirst to catch fish with its distinctive long, pointed bill.

Swifts, as well, are almost always airborne. They look similar to swallows, but they are not related at all. Their similarities are reflective of their ability to catch insects in flight, but in reality swifts are related to the hummingbird (see page 104). Swifts also seem like they have no feet, because they never settle on the ground; they only perch on vertical surfaces.

Belted Kingfisher
Ceryle alcyon

female

male

Length: 11–14 in.

What to look for: shaggy crest; bill heavy, sharp-pointed; blue-gray above, with blue-gray breast band (additional chestnut band on female).

Habitat: shores of lakes, ponds, streams; coasts.

As it leaves a favored perch overlooking a pool or lake, the belted kingfisher often utters its rattling call. Still calling, it dashes over the water, keeping its head slightly raised as if it were trying to see just a bit farther. It may fish by swooping close to the surface, dipping for its prey. Or it may climb to a considerable height, hold there on beating wings with head cocked, and then plunge. Kingfishers usually nest in a burrow in a steep bank, preferably near water. The tunnel may be as long as 15 feet, ending in a slightly elevated nest chamber.

White-throated Swift

Aeronautes saxatalis

Length: 6–7 in.

What to look for: black-and-white pattern on underside; long wings; notched tail.

Habitat: open air over rocky areas, especially canyons and mountains.

The fast-flying "rock swift" of the western mountains roosts and nests in crevices of cliffs, especially those overlooking deep canyons. A single crevice may contain a number of roosting swifts; at sunset a procession will stream in and disappear into the face of the cliff with incredible accuracy and speed. Vaux's swift *(Chaetura vauxi),* another western species, is smaller than the white-throated, with a grayish breast and shorter, unnotched tail.

Chimney Swift

Chaetura pelagica

Length: 4–5 in.

What to look for: small size; dark gray, lighter on throat; bow-shaped wings; short tail; body looks cigar-shaped in flight.

Habitat: open air over woodlands, farmlands, towns, cities.

Until man provided chimneys, wells, and other alternative sites, this dark little bird nested in hollow trees. Chimney swifts pass much of their lives in flight, beating their wings rapidly or holding them stiffly as they sail. They utter a distinctive series of high-pitched chips. No one knew where chimney swifts wintered until quite recently, when it was discovered that the entire population migrates to a remote part of the upper Amazon.

Feathered fact

Except when nesting or roosting, chimney swifts never perch anywhere; they are true denizens of the air.

flycatchers

There are several families of flycatchers, but the tyrant, seen throughout North America, is considered the largest family of birds on Earth, with around 430 known species. Because of this, these birds vary in shape, color, and pattern, so they are more difficult to identify than any other bird. Most perch quietly in the trees and sit upright on exposed branches, ready to snap up flying insects—hence, its name.

Scissor-tailed Flycatcher
Tyrannus forficatus

Feathered fact

This elegant bird's most notable feature is its deeply forked tail that opens and closes—scissor-style—while in flight.

Length: 11–15½ in.

What to look for: tail deeply forked, with extremely long feathers; pale gray above, with small rose shoulder patch; whitish below, shading to pink on flanks, belly, and underwings; immature less pink, with shorter tail.

Habitat: open brushy areas with scattered trees, poles, wires, or other high perches.

The male scissor-tailed flycatcher shows off in a remarkable courtship flight. Flying up to perhaps 100 feet above the ground, he begins a series of short, abrupt dives and climbs, ending the sequence by falling into two or three consecutive somersaults. Scissor-tails hunt insects from elevated perches and on the ground, seemingly unencumbered by their long tails. Adults of both sexes have the long, streaming plumes.

Olive-sided Flycatcher

Contopus borealis

Length: 6–7½ in.

What to look for: grayish brown above, white below, with brown-streaked sides; white patch below wing sometimes visible.

Habitat: coniferous and mixed woodlands, forest-edged bogs, swamps with dead trees; eucalyptus groves *(California)*.

Perched on top of a tall tree or dead snag, the olive-sided flycatcher whistles a cheery *pip-whee-beer.* The first note, *pip,* is inaudible at a distance, but the rest of the song is high and clear. When alarmed, this husky flycatcher calls *pip-pip-pip-pip.* The greater pewee *(Contopus pertinax)* of the southwestern mountains resembles the olive-sided but lacks the streaked sides and white patches.

Eastern Phoebe

Sayornis phoebe

Length: 5–7 in.

What to look for: brownish olive above, with darker head; whitish below, with gray breast; sits upright on perch and wags tail frequently.

Habitat: woodlands, farmlands, suburbs; usually near water.

Fibrit, says the eastern phoebe emphatically from its perch, wagging its tail in characteristic motion. Phoebes are not shy. Often they are found in or on porches, garages, barns, and bridges, nesting on a ledge or beam. This species made ornithological history in 1803 when Audubon tied silver thread on the legs of nestlings—the first North American experiment in bird banding. The next year he found that two of his marked birds had returned and were nesting nearby.

Yellow-bellied Flycatcher
Empidonax flaviventris

Length: 4½–5½ in.

What to look for: small size; brownish olive above, yellow below, with yellow throat; yellowish eye ring; whitish wingbars.

Habitat: northern coniferous forests, bogs; alder thickets, mixed woodlands (migration).

A bird of the wet northern forests, the yellow-bellied flycatcher nests on the ground or not far above it, in the side of a moss-covered bank or in the fern-draped earth clinging to the roots of a fallen tree. Its song is an upward-sliding *chee-weep,* sweet and melancholy; it also utters a short killick. In breeding plumage this species shows more yellow than any of its relatives in its range—the least (below), the willow *(Empidonax traillii),* or the alder *(Empidonax alnorum).* The Acadian flycatcher *(Empidonax virescens)* is a southeastern species, but it too is a bird of wet woods and streamsides, and on migration may be found in the same places as the yellow-bellied.

Least Flycatcher *Empidonax minimus*

Length: 4½–5 in.

What to look for: small size; belly white or pale yellow; head and back olive-gray; whitish eye ring and wingbars.

Habitat: open forests, orchards, rural towns, suburbs, parks.

The least flycatcher is noisy during the breeding season. Its curt *chebec* is given as often as 75 times a minute, and it may go on repeating itself for several hours at a time. The male sometimes adds a warble—*chebec-trree-treo, chebec-treee-chou.* Other notes include one-syllable *whit* calls. The species nests in both conifers and deciduous trees, usually quite low but at times as high as 60 feet. The deep little cup is frequently nestled in the crotch of a limb; materials include shreds of bark, plant down, spiderweb, fine woody stems, and grasses. Southerly nesters may raise two broods a year.

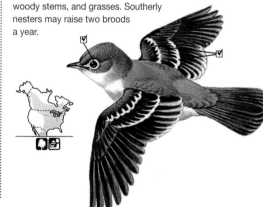

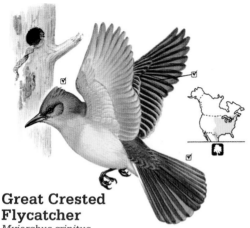

Great Crested Flycatcher
Myiarchus crinitus

Length: 7–9 in.

What to look for: reddish-brown tail and wing patch; yellow belly; whitish wingbars; slight crest.

Habitat: forests, clusters of trees.

This handsome bird announces its presence with a loud, clear *wheep* or rolling *crrreep*. The great crested flycatcher always nests in a cavity—an abandoned woodpecker hole, a hollow tree, or a nest box. If the hole is too deep, the birds will fill it up from the bottom with debris before beginning the nest of twigs. They may add a cast-off snakeskin or a strip of shiny plastic, which is sometimes left hanging outside the cavity. In dry parts of the West the smaller, ash-throated flycatcher *(Myiarchus cinerascens)* often nests in a hole in a large cactus.

Western Flycatcher
Empidonax difficilisloccidentalis

Length: 5–6 in.

What to look for: yellow throat and belly; olive-brown back; whitish eye ring and wingbars.

Habitat: moist coniferous and mixed forests, deciduous groves, wooded canyons.

Scientists have decided that the western flycatcher is actually two species separated by geography, the Pacific-slope *(Empidonax difficilis)* of the coast and Cordilleran *(Empidonax occidentalis)* of the Rockies. The green moss nest of the western flycatcher, lined with shredded bark, is always located in damp woods—often near a stream and sometimes even under the lip of a streambank. (It may also build as high as 30 feet up in a tree.) Two close relatives of the western flycatcher are best identified by habitat. Hammond's flycatcher *(Empidonax hammondii)* breeds in high coniferous forests. The dusky flycatcher *(Empidonax oberholseri)* is a bird of the foothill chaparral and of brushy mountain slopes.

male

female

Vermilion Flycatcher
Pyrocephalus rubinus

Length: 5–6 in.

What to look for: male with brilliant red cap and under-parts, dark brown back, wings, and tail; female brown above, light below, with fine streaking and pink wash on sides.

Habitat: wooded streamsides in arid regions; groves near water.

The courting male is very conspicuous as he circles up on rapidly beating wings, pausing often to give his tinkling song. He may climb as high as 50 feet before swooping down to perch near his mate. The nest, usually built into a horizontal crotch of a willow or mesquite, is a flat saucer of twigs, weeds, hair, and feathers, tied down with spider silk.

Eastern Wood-pewee
Contopus virens

Length: 5–6 in.

What to look for: brownish olive above, whitish below; conspicuous white wingbars; no eye ring.

Habitat: mature deciduous forests, other woodlands; especially along rivers.

Pee-a-wee, this bird whistles, sliding down, then up in pitch. Next it pauses and adds a downward-slurred *pee-ur.* During daylight a male pewee repeats this song every 5 or 10 seconds. But before dawn and after sunset, it sings even more frequently and adds the phrase *ah-di-day*—three ascending notes. The western wood-pewee *(Contopus sordidulus)* also has a "twilight song," ending in a rough *bzew.*

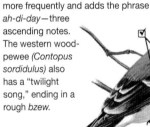

Feathered fact

Despite its abundance, the eastern wood-pewee is so indistinguishable that it could easily be overlooked if not for its relentless *pee-ah-wee* song.

attacking a crow

Eastern Kingbird *Tyrannus tyrannus*

Length: 7–9 in.

What to look for: blackish above, white below; dark tail, with prominent white band at tip; flies with stiff, shallow wingbeats from a high perch.

Habitat: forest edges; woodlands and open areas with occasional tall trees.

Thoreau called this flycatcher a "lively bird" and wrote that its noisy twittering "stirs and keeps the air brisk." The eastern kingbird is not only lively, it is fearless in defense of its territory. It will attack any passing crow or hawk, flying at it from above, pecking at the victim and pulling out feathers; it may even land on the flying intruder. The gray kingbird *(Tyrannus dominicensis)* is a slightly larger and paler bird of Florida and nearby coastal areas. Its bill is large, and it has no band on its notched tail.

Provide Additional Perching Areas

Flycatchers, such as the eastern kingbird, usually fly out from exposed perches to capture insects on the wing and then return to the perch to eat. Hummingbirds head for perches to digest nectar between binges. Others dart for a perch when predators come around. If perches are lacking in your yard, provide some additional ones yourself. Here are some tips:

Think about how the birds see your garden. When they first approach, they're likely to stop first in a high perch with good visibility of the entire area. From this vantage point, they will study your yard for predators and other birds that are defending their territory. If the coast is clear, they'll move down a few branches or to a fence to take a closer look. The birds will land on a feeder or the ground in your garden only after they have assured themselves that they are completely safe.

Some perches should be moderately high, 12 to 20 feet above the ground and offer unobstructed views of your yard. Trees are the most common high perches, though a nearby roof can serve the same purpose, as can tensioned cable installed between posts. In addition, provide places for the birds to land at different heights. Besides your tall perches, place several at heights of 6 to 8 feet and others at 3 to 4 feet.

Provide perches near feeders as well as water features to give birds a quick escape should any predators approach. Feeders and water features are frequently visited by birds from nearby perches and, like perches, should be placed so birds have an unobstructed view of the entire area. This way, they'll have time to react to danger.

Say's Phoebe
Sayornis saya

Length: 6–7½ in.

What to look for: lower breast and belly rusty; upperparts grayish; tail blackish; wags tail.

Habitat: open desert, semiarid areas, ranchlands, brushy fields, canyon mouths.

This dry-country flycatcher replaces the eastern phoebe in much of the West and has similar habits. It is a tail wagger, and it often nests on or around ranch buildings. Its call, however, is different—a low, plaintive *phee-eur.* Its customary perch is on top of a small bush, a tall weed stalk, or a low rock. In the northern portion of its range, Say's phoebe is migratory, but it is a year-round resident in warmer areas.

Western Kingbird *Tyrannus verticalis*

Length: 7–9 in.

What to look for: outer tail feathers white; cap, nape, and back gray; throat white; underparts yellow.

Habitat: arid open areas with scattered trees or tall brush; wooded stream valleys; farmlands.

This species, like other flycatchers, hunts from a perch. It flies out, plucks an insect from the air, and then sails back, often to the same spot. Adults teach their young to hunt by catching insects, disabling them, and releasing them for the young to fetch. A similar western species is Cassin's kingbird *(Tyrannus vociferans),* with a darker breast and no white outer tail feathers.

swallows and larks

Creatures of the air that feast on insects captured in flight, swallows are superbly equipped for this very special way of life. Their bills are short and wide, opening and closing with precise snaps; their wings are long, narrow, and pointed to reduce the wasting drag of friction; and their notched or deeply forked tail facilitates fast turns in pursuit of prey.

Like the swallow, the horned lark prefers wide-open spaces, soaring to heights of up to 800 feet, but what makes this feathered gem distinctive from all others is its ability to bellow sweet, melodious songs in high display.

immature

Barn Swallow
Hirundo rustica

Length: 5½–7 in.

What to look for:
tail deeply forked; glossy dark blue above; light rufous below, with darker throat.

Habitat: open woodlands, other open areas, farmlands, suburbs.

Like the cliff swallow, this species has benefited from man's constructions, building its mud nest in culverts, under wharves and bridges, and inside sheds, garages, and barns. The barn swallow feeds almost entirely on insects, which it picks out of the air in its swift, graceful flight; often it will dart close to the surface of a pond, splashing itself from time to time. Before the start of the fall migration, barn swallows join with other swallow species to form huge flocks that rest and preen on telephone wires.

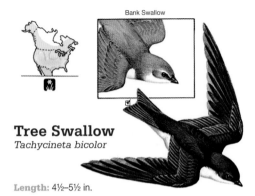

Bank Swallow

Tree Swallow
Tachycineta bicolor

Length: 4½–5½ in.

What to look for: glossy blue-black or greenish above (immature dark brown), white below; tail slightly forked.

Habitat: open areas with scattered trees and dead stubs; usually near water.

This is the hardiest swallow, arriving early in spring and even wintering over in some localities. When insects are unavailable, tree swallows feed mostly on bayberries; some wintering birds have also been seen picking seeds from pond ice. Tree swallows will nest in birdhouses and mailboxes, as well as in holes in dead tree stubs, their natural nesting sites. In fall the brown-backed immatures can be mistaken for bank swallows *(Riparia riparia),* which have brown "collars," and for rough-winged swallows *(Stelgidopteryx serripennis),* which have a brown wash on the throat. In the West, adult birds can be confused with violet-green swallows *(Tachycineta thalassina),* a species with more white on the lower back.

Cliff Swallow *Hirundo pyrrhonota*

Length: 5–6 in.

What to look for: mostly dark above; light forehead; rusty rump and throat; square tail.

Habitat: open country cliffs, farmlands with bridges or buildings for nesting; usually near water.

After it was reported from Hudson Bay in 1772, no naturalist noticed the cliff swallow—or mentioned it, anyway—until 1815, when Audubon found a few in Kentucky. From then on, the birds were seen in many parts of North America. Probably they had simply been overlooked all those years. Quite likely, cliff swallows began appearing where people could get a look at them as they gradually discovered the suitability of nest sites under the eaves of houses and barns (cliffsides are their natural nest sites). These are the swallows that return to the Mission of San Juan Capistrano, in California, on or about March 19 each year.

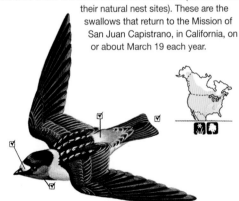

female

male

Purple Martin *Progne subis*

Length: 7–8 in.

What to look for: largest swallow; tail slightly forked; male glossy blue-black; female duller above, with mottled throat and whitish belly.

Habitat: open areas, scattered woodlands, farmlands, suburbs; usually near water.

Purple martins have a long history of nesting in shelters supplied by man. In the past they used hollow gourds hung by Indians, and today the species is largely dependent on martin houses. These birds have a strong homing instinct, demonstrated by a colony that returned one spring to find its apartment house gone. The martins hovered and circled at the precise spot in midair where the house had been.

Horned Lark *Eremophila alpestris*

Length: 6–7½ in.

What to look for: chest and head patterned with black and yellow; black tail with white on outside; "horns" not always visible.

Habitat: stony deserts, tundra, grasslands, other open spaces, shore areas.

The horned lark is a bird of the bare earth, where it nests and feeds, and the sky, where it soars, sings, and plummets downward once again. In the fall individuals from the far North migrate in large flocks, joining the local breeding birds wherever they find their preferred habitat—ground with a minimum of low vegetation to supply the seeds on which they feed. This is North America's only true lark.

prairie race

northern race

woodpeckers and nuthatches

These wood-boring birds possess an exceptionally long tongue and chiseled bills for snatching insects from the bark of trees. While woodpeckers and sapsuckers rely on their stiff, spiny tail to prop them up when climbing trees, the nuthatch doesn't need to rely on this special equipment; these small, stubby climbers go down trees headfirst.

Pileated Woodpecker
Dryocopus pileatus

Length: 14–18½ in.

What to look for: large size; red crest; black, white, and red pattern on head; mostly black, with white wing linings conspicuous in flight

Habitat: mature forests.

The slow, rhythmic hammering of a pileated woodpecker may be mistaken for the sound of a man chopping down a tree. With powerful whacks the bird digs a large rectangular or oval hole deep into the heart of a tree infested with carpenter ants, a principal food. Fresh chips at the base of a tree indicate a hole that is still being dug.

male

female

Feathered fact
The title of largest North American woodpecker now goes to the magnificent pileated.

Acorn Woodpecker

Melanerpes formicivorus

Length: 8½–9½ in.

What to look for: red, black, and white pattern on head and neck; upper parts mostly black, with white wing patch and rump.

Habitat: stands of oak, mixed woodlands, canyons, foothills with scattered trees.

The acorn-storing woodpecker, as it used to be called, drills small holes in trees and packs them with nuts (usually acorns), one to each hole. One packed ponderosa pine was studded with an estimated 50,000 acorns. The acorn woodpecker is remarkable, too, for its breeding habits. Unlike other woodpeckers, it is very social and often nests in colonies of a dozen or so. Several pairs may even share in digging a nest hole and then cooperate in incubating the eggs and raising the young.

Red-bellied Woodpecker

Melanerpes carolinus

Length: 8–10 in.

What to look for: fine black-and-white barring on back; red nape; red crown (male); white patch near end of wings visible in flight.

Habitat: forests, groves, orchards, farmlands, suburbs.

This abundant southern species is now expanding its range to the North. In the South the red-belly occasionally feeds on oranges, but it makes up for this by eating quantities of destructive insects. It most often nests in a dead tree at the edge of a woodland, frequently using the same hole year after year. The female lays unspotted white eggs, usually four or five in a clutch. (This is typical of woodpeckers.) The name red-bellied woodpecker is misleading, for the red patch on its belly is rather faint.

Red-headed Woodpecker

Melanerpes erythrocephalus

Length: 7–10 in.

What to look for: red head and neck; mostly black and white, with large white wing patches; immature brownish on head and back.

Habitat: open woods, groves, swamps with dead trees.

The diet of the red-headed woodpecker is notably varied. It includes beechnuts, acorns, corn, fruits, insects, and the eggs and young of small birds. Like several other woodpeckers, this species has the habit of storing food for future use. Grasshoppers are stuffed into crevices in fence posts, and nuts are packed into knotholes and into cracks in buildings. Wherever nut trees are abundant and productive, there is a good chance of seeing this woodpecker and hearing its loud *quee-o, quee-o, queer.*

Three-toed Woodpecker

Picoides tridactylus

Length: 7–9 in.

What to look for: yellow crown (male); back with black and white bars or jagged white patch; barred sides; wings mostly black.

Habitat: coniferous forests.

The three-toed woodpecker is an unusual bird. It is the only woodpecker that lives both in North America and Eurasia. It has two toes pointing forward, one pointing backward. Except for the similar black-backed woodpecker, *Picoides arcticus,* other woodpeckers have four toes. Males of both species have yellow head patches, not red. And instead of hammering into trees, as most woodpeckers do, they flake off sheets of bark from dead trees and feed on the wood borers and beetles underneath.

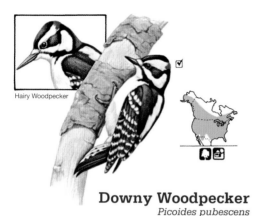

Hairy Woodpecker

Downy Woodpecker
Picoides pubescens

Length: 5–6½ in.

What to look for: small size; short bill; black-and-white pattern on head and wings; white back; red patch on head (male).

Habitat: woodlands, orchards, suburbs, parks.

The little downy is probably our most familiar woodpecker. In winter it readily takes suet from bird feeders and often joins the mixed bands of small birds that roam through the woods, each species feeding in a different manner but all deriving protection from the wariness of the flock. The larger, hairy woodpecker *(Picoides villosus)* is more of a forest dweller than the downy. Both "downies" and "hairies" are named for their feathers, probably the short ones around their nostrils.

Yellow-bellied Sapsucker
Sphyrapicus varius

Length: 7–8½ in.

What to look for: long white wing stripe; black, white, and red pattern on head and neck; immature brownish, with wing stripe.

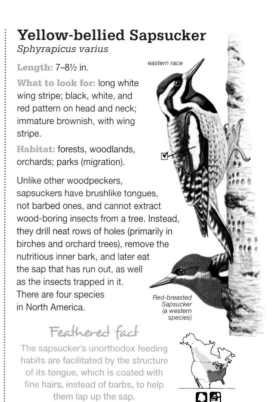

eastern race

Habitat: forests, woodlands, orchards; parks (migration).

Unlike other woodpeckers, sapsuckers have brushlike tongues, not barbed ones, and cannot extract wood-boring insects from a tree. Instead, they drill neat rows of holes (primarily in birches and orchard trees), remove the nutritious inner bark, and later eat the sap that has run out, as well as the insects trapped in it. There are four species in North America.

Red-breasted Sapsucker (a western species)

Feathered fact
The sapsucker's unorthodox feeding habits are facilitated by the structure of its tongue, which is coated with fine hairs, instead of barbs, to help them lap up the sap.

red-shafted race

yellow-shafted race

Northern Flicker
Colaptes auratus

Length: 10–13 in.

What to look for: white rump; black crescent at throat; yellow or red on underside of wings and tail (in East, yellow only); male with "mustache" of black (East) or red (West).

Habitat: deserts, farmlands, suburbs, parks, open forests.

This unusual woodpecker is often seen on the ground, searching for ants and licking them up with its long tongue. It does, however, nest in holes in trees—or tree substitutes such as telephone poles. Flickers are conspicuous in fall, when they often travel in loose flocks. In spring their arrival is announced by noisy calls—*wick-a, wick-a, wick-a.*

Brown Creeper
Certhia americana

Length: 4½–5½ in.

What to look for: streaked brown above, write below; bill long, slender, curved down.

Habitat: mixed and coniferous forests, groves, woods.

The spring song of the brown creeper is a high, sweet phrase, surprisingly different from its usual thin *sssst.* But since the spring song is ventriloquistic, the bird can be difficult to locate. In feeding the brown creeper invariably flies to the bottom

of a tree and gradually hitches its way up the trunk in its search for insects. Then it drops to the bottom of another tree and begins hitching upward once again.

Feathered fact

The brown creeper begins its climb at the base of a large tree. It creeps swiftly upward with peculiar jerking movements, going around and around the trunk in a loose spiral until it almost reaches the top. Then it just lets go and lands at the base of the next tree and starts all over again.

White-breasted Nuthatch
Sitta carolinensis

Length: 5–6 in.

What to look for: black crown and nape; blue-gray above, white below; bill long, straight.

Habitat: mixed and deciduous forests, woods; groves; suburbs.

The nuthatches are the only birds that habitually climb down tree trunks headfirst, gathering insects and insect eggs from crevices and under the bark. The name nuthatch derives from nut-hack, for the way the birds wedge nuts and other food into crevices and chop them into pieces. The southeastern brown-headed nuthatch *(Sitta pusilla)* and the western pygmy nuthatch *(Sitta pygmaea)* are smaller species.

Red-breasted Nuthatch
Sitta canadensis

Length: 3½–4½ in.

What to look for: white line above eye; black cap; blue-gray back; reddish underparts.

Habitat: coniferous forests; mixed woodlands (mainly in winter).

The red-breasted nuthatch usually digs its nest hole in dead wood, but it may also use natural cavities, old woodpecker holes, and nest boxes. Whatever site it chooses, it always smears the entrance hole with pitch from spruce, fir, or pine, perhaps to discourage predators. This nuthatch is an active little bird, scurrying over tree trunks and branches, dashing from tree to tree, and calling *yna, yna, yna, yna* in a thin, nasal voice. The White-breasted species has a lower-pitched call.

The Nuthatch: An Upside-Down Little Bird

Although nuthatches and woodpeckers share the same role of gleaning insects from the trunks and larger limbs of trees, their different styles permit a happy division of the bounty. Woodpeckers, braced back on their tails, hop up the tree, while nuthatches move downward, spotting whatever beetles and other insects might have been missed by the woodpecker.

Their toes are unusually long and so are their down-turned claws. The tiny hooks at the tips catch easily into the slightest roughness, allowing the birds to run helter-skelter as they search for insects, looking more like a windup toy than a live bird. True to his name, the nuthatch also enjoys nuts and can be seen in winter foraging for acorns, hickory nuts, and other seeds.

hummingbirds

Hummingbirds are among the most fascinating of all the passerines because of their extraordinary ability to hover in midair with a wing-beat rate of 20 to 25 beats per second. They also have the highest metabolism of any bird, and they consume more than their weight in nectar every day. To do this, they continuously feed on flowers, drinking the sweet nectar with their long, pointed bills and grooved troughlike tongues.

Many believe that hummingbirds spend almost all day flying. But in actuality, they spend more than half their day sitting and digesting the nectar and small insects they consume.

Fortunately, these striking birds are easy to attract. Just plant some red nectar-producing flowers, provide some sugar-water solution, and set out a banana peel or two to attract some small insects, and they'll be gracing your yard in no time.

hummingbirds

Active, colorful, and endlessly engaging, hummingbirds are exciting to watch as they hover incessantly above a flower or fly at breakneck speed to defend their territory against a rival songbird. Many males have coats of iridescent, nearly fluorescent feathers, with bright spots under their bills. The females are more muted, but at times they too sparkle with color when the light strikes their backs and rapidly beating wings.

Hummingbirds are creatures of habit and rely on sight to find food sources, so if they chance upon your feeder and like what they find, they will most likely become a backyard regular.

Anna's Hummingbird
Calypte anna

Length: 3–4 in.

What to look for: bill long, slender; metallic green above; iridescent dark red crown and throat (male); white-tipped tail (female).

Habitat: open woodlands; chaparral; suburban and city gardens.

When the female Anna's hummingbird lays her eggs, her nest may be only half finished; she completes it while incubating. Like most hummingbird nests, it consists of tiny stems and plant down, held together and lashed to a branch with spider silk and often camouflaged with bits of lichen. A female feeds her young without any help from her mate. She collects nectar, tree sap, insects, and spiders, and delivers the meal by thrusting her long bill deep down the nestlings' throats.

Black-chinned Hummingbird

Archilochus alexandri

Length: 3–3¾ in.

What to look for: back metallic green; throat black, bordered with iridescent purple (male); slightly forked tail.

Habitat: dry scrub, woodlands near streams, wooded canyons, mountain meadows, gardens.

Hummingbirds are unique to the New World. European explorers were astounded by the tiny glittering creatures that zipped up and down, backward and sideways, with wings humming and blurred. Hummingbirds perform set figures in courtship flights. The male black-chinned hummingbird, for instance, swings in pendulumlike arcs above the female; at the top of each swoop, he comes to a dead stop and taps his wings together underneath his body.

Creating a Natural Hummingbird Haven

Placing sugar-water feeders around your yard will surely attract a bounty of hummingbirds, but there are also a number of beautiful plants and bushes that will lure them as well—providing both natural food and a beautiful backdrop in which to enjoy these stunning creatures.

Below are some of the best trees, bushes, vines, and flowers for attracting hummingbirds. Check with your local garden center to see which thrive best in your area. Selecting a variety of plants that flower at different times will ensure a steady stream of visitors throughout the season.

Trees and Shrubs
- azalea
- butterfly bush
- cape honeysuckle
- flame Aacanthus
- flowering quince
- lantana
- manzanita
- mimosa
- red buckeye
- tree tobacco
- Turk's cap
- weigela

Vines
- coral honeysuckle
- cypress vine
- morning glory
- scarlet runner bean
- trumpet creeper

Perennials
- bee balm
- canna
- cardinal flower
- columbine
- coral bells
- four o'clocks
- foxglove
- hosta
- hummingbird mint
- yucca

Annuals
- firespike
- fuchsia
- impatiens
- Jacobiana
- jewelweed
- petunia
- salvia

How to Prepare a Sugar-Water Solution

Offering hummingbirds a refined sugar-water solution as a substitute for flower nectar is an excellent way to help fuel their astonishing metabolism. This is especially important when flowers aren't in bloom, such as during migration.

You can offer sugar water simply by hanging recycled yogurt cups filled with the solution, or you can buy commercial nectar feeders.

To prepare a sterile and safe sugar-water solution, follow these simple steps:

- Boil one part refined white sugar to four parts boiling water. (Do not use honey, brown sugar, or food coloring. These can be harmful to the birds.)

- Mix until the sugar is completely dissolved.

- Cover the solution and allow it to cool.

- Before filling your feeder, wash it with soap and hot water. Rinse thoroughly.

- Tie a red ribbon to your feeder to catch the hummingbirds' attention, and hang the feeder in a sunny, open area with nearby trees for perching.

Any leftover sugar water should be stored in your refrigerator and must be used within two weeks. In hot weather, especially, sugar water can spoil. Be sure to change your water weekly (see "Maintaining Sugar-Water Feeders," opposite).

Rufous Hummingbird
Selasphorus rufus

Length: 3½–4 in.

What to look for: male mostly red-brown, with iridescent orange-red throat and sides of head; female with green back, rufous on flanks and base of tail feathers.

Habitat: alpine meadows, edges of woodlands; lowlands (migration).

The rufous hummingbird flies farther north than any other hummingbird. As the birds move south toward Mexico (mainly in July and August), they may be found as high in the mountains as 13,200 feet. Hummingbirds are generally feisty, but this species is particularly pugnacious. Yet at times rufous hummingbirds appear to breed in colonies, with some pairs nesting only a few feet from one another. The similar-looking Allen's hummingbird *(Selasphorus sasin),* which occurs along the West Coast from Oregon south, has a green back and cap.

Feathered fact
Rufous hummingbirds are migrants. When the calendar says it's midsummer, the rufous are already far from their nesting grounds in Montana and western Washington and on the way to their winter quarters in Mexico.

Ruby-throated Hummingbird
Archilochus colubris

Length: 3–3½ in.

What to look for: bill long, needlelike; metallic green above; throat metallic red (male) or dingy white (female).

Habitat: deciduous and mixed forests; rural, suburban, and city gardens.

Of the 15 species of hummingbird that regularly nest north of Mexico, this is the only one breeding east of the Great Plains. The broad-tailed hummingbird *(Selasphorus platycercus)* of western mountains is similar in appearance, but the ranges of the two do not overlap. "Hummers," unlike other birds, can fly backward or straight up and down. They can also hover and are able to drink flower nectar without actually landing on the blossom. The flowers they drink from are usually long, tubular, and orange or red.

Feathered fact

The ruby-throated hummingbird has the highest metabolism of any warm-blooded vertebrate in the world, except perhaps the shrew. Just to stay alive, it must eat all day long.

Maintaining Sugar-Water Feeders

Hummingbird feeders have tiny feeding holes, and crawling insects, such as ants, easily find their way in, leading to spoilage. In addition, birds that visit feeders leave behind bacteria, fungi, and yeast cells. Within days the sugar-water solution ferments or begins to grow mold. If this happens, hummingbirds will quickly abandon your feeders and look for a more reliable food source.

Here's how you can avoid these problems:

- Clean the feeder every three days in warm weather and every five days when temperatures are cool.

- Empty and wash the feeder's interior and exterior with hot, soapy water. Use a bottle brush or wire probe.

- Rinse the feeder in clean water to remove soap residue.

- Follow up with a sterilizing solution of water and bleach.

- Soak the feeder and all of its parts in bleach solution for a half hour, rinse thoroughly, and wipe it dry.

- Finally, allow it to air dry for 15 minutes before refilling it with sterile sugar-water solution (see "How to Prepare a Sugar-Water Solution," opposite).

other birds

Varied in their habits and habitats, the distinctive birds on these next few pages are a delight to watch. Each one is a master of its own way of life: the swift, fearless, and powerful great horned owl, equipped with powerful talons for striking and gripping prey; the shameless, opportunistic burrowing owl, happy to take over abandoned woodpecker holes, hawk nests, and even armadillo dens; the slender, secretive cuckoo, most often heard and never seen; the sleek, quick-footed, snake-eating roadrunner, agile enough to dodge coyotes; the unobtrusive and graceful plump-bodied dove.

All are integral elements of the American landscape, irreplaceable gems in our wildlife heritage.

doves

Doves and wild pigeons are commonly grouped together. In fact, mourning doves, the most common of the species, are also referred to as gray wild pigeons. They prefer open land and to get their water from streams, but because they are fast flyers and travel easily, they will gladly fly several miles from their nest to visit backyard feeders. They also rely on their fast speed to escape predators. But when it comes to their young, they are even more crafty: If predators and people come too close to their nestlings, they've been known to crash-land, faking injury to lure predators away.

Rock Dove (Pigeon)
Columba livia

Length: 11–14 in.

What to look for: usually gray, with purplish neck, white rump, and black-banded tail; sometimes white, brown, black, or mixed.

Habitat: cities, towns, farms.

The rock dove, originally from Europe and Asia, nests on cliffs in the wild and has easily adapted to the ledges of human buildings. rock doves breed several times a year, beginning in March, when the males' ardent cooing is one of the sounds of spring. A mated pair shares the incubation and care of the young, which are fed on regurgitated "pigeon's milk," a secretion from the bird's crop. Breeders have developed several color strains, but free-living flocks usually contain many gray birds with iridescent necks, similar to the original wild rock doves.

Mourning Dove *Zenaida macroura*

Length: 10–12 in.

What to look for: slim body; tail long, pointed, edged with white; grayish brown above, with scattered black spots.

Habitat: deserts, brushy areas, woodlands, farmlands, suburbs, parks.

The mourning dove's mellow, vaguely melancholy call—*coo-ah, coo, coo, coo*—is repeated again and again, sliding upward on the second syllable and then down for the last three notes. Mourning doves build a flimsy nest of sticks, usually in an evergreen tree close to the trunk. Two eggs make a set. The parents share incubating duties, the male sitting much of the day and his mate during the night. The young are fed by regurgitation, then gradually weaned to insects and the adults' main food, seeds.

Common Ground-Dove
Columbina passerina

Length: 5–6½ in.

What to look for: small size; tail short, rounded; wings with brownish-red patches visible in flight.

Habitat: deserts, dry grasslands, open woodlands, farmlands.

The plump little common ground-dove is the smallest of our doves, about the size of a house sparrow. As it walks along, hunting for seeds, it nods its head (as do other members of its family). This is a tame species and will permit a close approach. Usually it flies for only a short distance, showing bright reddish-brown patches on its wings. In its southern habitat the ground-dove favors sandy or weedy areas, cotton fields, and citrus groves. The southwestern Inca dove *(Columbina inca)* somewhat resembles the ground-dove but has a long, narrow tail edged with white, like that of a mourning dove.

doves   111

cuckoos

American cuckoos can't actually sing, but the unusual sounds they make so often precede summer storms that for generations these birds have been called "rain crows." These slender birds are so secretive they are seldom seen. Slipping furtively among the trees, they fly briefly across clearings with swift and purposeful grace.

But the greater roadrunner, the largest of the North American cuckoos, couldn't be more opposite. This sprightly wild creature is so named because it darts across roads and fearlessly approaches humans with a curious eye, raising its crest at a jaunty angle and attracting attention wherever it goes.

Yellow-billed Cuckoo
Coccyzus americanus

Length: 10½–12½ in.

What to look for: long, slim bird; gray-brown above, white below; underside of tail black, with 3 pairs of large white spots; yellow lower mandible; reddish brown wing patches visible in flight.

Habitat: moist second-growth woodlands; brushy areas near water.

Unlike some cuckoos, the yellow-billed does not regularly lay its eggs in other birds' nests—but it is not much of a nest maker, either. The structure of sticks, rootlets, grass, and leaves are shallow and loosely built, and often appear to be too small for a sitting bird and her eggs. From the moment the chicks are hatched almost to the day they fly, they are covered with quills, like miniature porcupines. Then the quills burst open and the feathers bloom out. This species and the similar black-billed cuckoo *(Coccyzuz erythropthalmus),* common in the East, are as inconspicuous in behavior as in plumage. They slip noiselessly from branch to branch, uttering an occasional *cuk-cuk-cuk.*

Greater Roadrunner

Geococcyx californianus

Length: 20–24 in.

What to look for: large size; long tail; rough crest; patch of red and pale blue behind eye; runs rapidly but seldom flies.

Habitat: deserts, semiarid areas with scattered brush and trees.

The roadrunner is really a ground-dwelling cuckoo, though it neither looks nor behaves like a cuckoo. This long-tailed, long-legged bird is very agile and fast on its feet; one was clocked at 15 miles an hour. The roadrunner is famous for feeding on snakes—poisonous or otherwise—and lizards. It also eats scorpions, spiders, grasshoppers, crickets, small mammals, birds' eggs, and even small birds that it catches in flight by leaping into the air and snatching them with its bill. Most items are simply swallowed, but a big lizard, for instance, is softened by being beaten on a rock. The roadrunner is not a quiet bird. It crows and chuckles. It rolls its mandibles together, producing a clacking sound. And mostly it coos like a dove–a most unusual cuckoo altogether.

Why Everyone Goes Cuckoo over This Extraordinary Bird

There are many unusual birds in North America known for their extraordinary feats. Take, for instance, the gregarious belted kingfisher. Quick and deadly, this aggressive loner dives headfirst into the water in pursuit of prey. Or the ruby-throated hummingbird. Ruthlessly territorial, this eloquent creature spars with bumblebees for flower rights.

These birds are indeed remarkable, but there is none more legendary than the greater roadrunner. Perhaps this wonderment lies in its speed, its whimsical look, its clownish gait, or the fact that it can catch and wrestle a rattlesnake—always emerging a winner. In fact, the roadrunner's quick-witted abilities are so theatrical, they were the basis for the Warner Bros. animated cartoon series *Wile E. Coyote and Road Runner.*

Here are some other amazing things you may not know about this desert ground dweller:

- The roadrunner kills a rattler by catching its tail in its mouth and repeatedly cracking the snake's head across a hard surface.

- To warm up, roadrunners turn their back to the sun, fluff their back feathers, and expose the black skin along their back to absorb the solar energy.

- Besides rattlesnakes, the greater roadrunner eats many other venomous prey items, including scorpions and tarantulas.

- It frequently captures small birds at bird feeders and nesting sites, leaping from nearby hiding spots.

owls

Owls are considered birds of prey and are closely related to hawks. Of the 160 species in the world today, nearly all are nocturnal, feeding on rodents, birds, reptiles, fish, and large insects. Owls are abundant, especially in wooded areas, but they are so elusive you may not even realize they are a regular backyard guest. If you ever see a regurgitated pellet of fur or bone on the ground, look up and you may spot an owl sitting in a nest. Another giveaway is the raucous sound of a flock of small songbirds; they often gang up on a roosting owl.

Feathered fact
This owl has been described as the "tiger of the woods" because of its superb nighttime hunting ability and flesh-tearing beak.

Great Horned Owl
Bubo virginianus

Length: 18–24 in.

What to look for: large size; widely spaced ear tufts; mottled brown above, lighter below, with fine dark barring.

Habitat: scrub areas, woodlands, deserts, canyons, bottomlands.

This daring and adaptable species, found virtually throughout the Americas, will attack any medium-sized mammal or bird—porcupine or skunk, duck or grouse. In North America the great horned owl begins to breed in the cold of winter. Two or three eggs are laid, usually in the old nest of a large hawk or crow, sometimes in a hollow tree or a cave. Calls are many and various, but the common one is a series of muffled hoots—*hoo, hoo-hoo, hoooo-hoo.* The male's voice is higher-pitched than the female's, and a pair in concert seem to harmonize, often in thirds.

Burrowing Owl *Speotyto cunicularia*

Length: 8–10½ in.

What to look for: round head; long legs; short tail; brown above, spotted with buff and white; paler below.

Habitat: prairies, plains, deserts, other open spaces.

Typically this owl is seen standing at the entrance to its burrow, bowing and bobbing in a comic way. In the West it nests in the abandoned burrows of prairie dogs. A burrow ordinarily slopes down for about 3 feet, then runs back horizontally to a nesting chamber 10 feet or more from the entrance. The birds line this chamber with feathers, grass, dried mammal dung, and the remains of prey. Five or six eggs make up the set, and both parents incubate and raise the young. These owls feed on insects, reptiles, and rodents, hunting during the day as well as in the evening.

Snowy Owl
Nyclea scandiaca

Length: 19–25 in.

What to look for: large size; mostly white, with dark flecks; active in daylight.

Habitat: tundra; prairies, open fields, marshes, beaches (winter).

Snowy owls nest on the tundra around the top of the globe. In winters when food (chiefly lemmings and hares) is scarce, large numbers move south to the northern United States. Snowy owls show little fear of human activities, and so it is not uncommon to see one perched on the roof of a building or on a highway sign beside an airport. The owls are usually silent in winter, but on their breeding grounds they hoot, whistle, rattle, and bark.

Long-eared Owl

Short-eared Owl
Asio flammeus

Length: 12–16 in.

What to look for: head rounded, dark areas on wing; mottled yellowish brown; flight erratic, flapping.

Habitat: tundra, brushy areas, prairies, dunes, marshes.

This is a bird of the open country. A daytime and twilight hunter, the short-eared owl will occasionally perch on a fencepost to spot its rodent prey, but usually it is seen coursing over a pasture or marsh. The range of the short-eared owl includes much of the Americas and Eurasia. The long-eared owl *(Asia otus)* has a similarly wide range. It is nocturnal, however, and nests in trees, not on the ground.

Barred Owl *Strix varia*

Length: 16–23 in.

What to look for: large round head; no ear tufts; dark eyes; mottled brown, with barred throat and streaked underparts.

Habitat: wet woodlands, wooded swamps, floodplains.

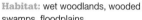

In the daytime an owl sitting inconspicuously in a tree is frequently mobbed by a noisy flock of scolding small birds— a sure tip-off to an owl watcher. The barred owl's far-carrying, rhythmic hooting, heard by day as well as night, is often written as *Who cooks for you? Who cooks for you-all?* The bird also gives a hair-raising catlike scream. The barred owl's larger and rarer relative, the great gray owl *(Strix nebulosa)*, breeds in northern and mountain forests but occasionally appears farther south and east during the winter.

Eastern Screech-Owl *Otus asio*

Length: 7–10 in.

What to look for: small size; ear tufts; reddish, brown, or gray; sometimes perches in tree holes.

Habitat: forests, groves, farmlands, towns, parks.

The call of this small owl is a series of mellow hoots or, more typically, a quavery, eerie wail. The screech owl's wail is not difficult for man to imitate, and such imitations may get dozens of curious or outraged small birds to respond. The western screech-owl (*Otus kennicottii),* of the western half of the continent, is almost identical, but its call is a series of soft notes, all on one pitch and speeding up at the end.

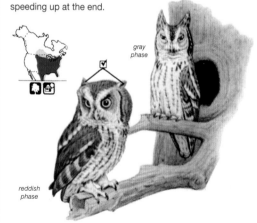

gray
phase

reddish
phase

Common Barn-Owl
Tyto alba

Length: 13–19 in.

What to look for: face heart-shaped, mostly white; golden brown above, usually white below; legs long, feathered; mothlike flight.

Habitat: forests near open country; farmlands, towns.

Long before this worldwide species was a "barn" owl, it nested in hollow trees, caves, and burrows. Often it still does. But man's structures furnish it with ideal cover, and the bird can be found in belfries, attics, and abandoned mines as well as barns. This owl is a nocturnal hunter. Experiments have shown that it requires its ears only to locate prey.

Index of Birds Profiled in This Book

Also available from Reader's Digest...

This handy little reference is the ideal book for anyone looking to attract backyard birds by making their own recipes using ingredients right from the kitchen. Provides expert advice on feeders, birdbaths, seasonal needs, nuisance critters, and plants and trees birds love—along with several do-it-yourself projects you can complete in an afternoon. An excellent resource for those looking to extend a special welcome to these backyard guests.

$9.95 • 120 pages • ISBN 978-1-60652-131-1

This indispensable, richly illustrated guide will help you turn your yard into a natural haven for birds and butterflies. Complete with an A-to-Z flower and plant directory; easy, clever projects; a field guide; and bird-watching basics, *Birds in Your Backyard* provides everything you need to know to create an irresistible garden and a welcoming backyard sanctuary.

$17.95 paperback • 272 pages • ISBN 978-0-7621-0997-5

Hundreds of handsome, original full-color paintings, coupled with informative essays, make this book fun to read, easy to use, informative, and lovely to look at. Includes at-a-glance information, range maps to show you where and when each species can be found, and the best spots for bird-watching across North America—the perfect book for anyone who loves nature.

$19.95 paperback • 576 pages • ISBN 978-0-7621-0576-2

Reader's Digest books can be purchased through retail and online bookstores.
In the United States books are distributed by Penguin Group (USA), Inc.
For more information or to order books, call 1-800-788-6262.